I BELIEVE

Y U

MATTER

A GUIDE TO EMOTIONAL INDEPENDENCE

RASESHA RABARI

ISBN
Paperback 979-8-89632-840-7
Hardcase 979-8-89632-955-8

Contents

Introduction

Your Emotions Want to Reach Out to You:

In a world filled with endless demands, comparisons, and pressures, our emotions often sit quietly in the background, waiting for us to notice them. But here's the truth—they're not just waiting; they're calling out to you, yearning for acknowledgment, for understanding, for healing. Your emotions want to reach out to you because they are the essence of your humanity, the compass of your life, and the bridge to your personal power.

You see, emotional health isn't a luxury—it's the foundation for a fulfilled life. Yet, we often treat our emotions like an inconvenience, something to suppress or control. But what if I told you that within every tear, every pang of anxiety, in every burst of frustration lies a message? A lesson? A chance to grow?

Let's face these together.
Why Support Is Important:

In my work and research, I've seen how deeply emotions shape our experiences. When ignored, they manifest as depression, anxiety, or chronic stress. When nurtured, they become stepping stones to resilience, empathy, and joy.

Recent studies reveal a stark reality:

Depression and persistent sadness now affect one in five people globally.

Anxiety isn't just about being "nervous"; it's a relentless loop of "what ifs" that can steal joy and stability.

Loneliness has become an epidemic, with social isolation impacting physical and mental health as much as smoking.

Burnout is no longer confined to high-achievers; it's a universal cry for balance in an overworked world.

These aren't just problems; they're signals that something deeper is at play. Our emotional health is screaming for attention, but we've been conditioned to silence it.

What's at Stake?

When we ignore our emotions, we allow self-doubt, fear, and frustration to take control. Have you ever felt trapped by the duality of your thoughts? That voice in your head saying, "You can't do this. You're not enough," while another part of you whispers, "But I want to try"? That inner conflict creates illusions—barriers that feel insurmountable. And trust me, I know how exhausting it is to battle those voices daily. It feels like swimming against the tide of your own mind. But let me tell you something crucial:

The only person who matters in this journey is you.

Not because of your achievements. Not because of your ambitions. But because you exist. Because you're still holding on despite the weight of it all. That alone is extraordinary.

The Gift of Emotional Freedom

What if I told you that freedom isn't about escaping pain but learning to live alongside it? Emotional freedom is the strength to face your feelings, understand their roots, and let them guide you instead of control you. It's not about perfection; it's about progress.

When you achieve emotional freedom, you stop living reactively. You stop basing your worth on others' opinions or external success. Instead, you root yourself in authenticity. Y ou discover that growth doesn't happen in comfort zones—it happens when you step into the unknown, even if it terrifies you.

You Matter—And Here's Why

Let me speak directly to your heart:

I know life hasn't always been kind. The weight of unmet expectations, the sting of rejection, the exhaustion of simply trying to "keep it together"—it's enough to make anyone want to give up. But here's what I want you to remember:

You're the hero of your story.

Your essence—the core of who you are—is not defined by your struggles. It's defined by your resilience. The fire inside you might feel like a flicker right now, but it hasn't gone out. And this book is your matchstick.

You're capable of more than you realize. But it starts with believing in yourself. Not because everything will suddenly become easy, but because you are worth the effort. Your freedom, your growth, and your peace are your birthright. And they're closer than you think.

It's time to break free from the cycles that hold you back. The cycles of self-doubt, procrastination, and fear. I know it's hard—it's supposed to be. Growth always feels like resistance at first. But trust me, it's worth it.

This book is not just a guide; it's a lifeline. A reminder that you're not alone, that you're not invisible, and that your struggles are valid. It's here for the moments when you feel like giving up, when the world feels too heavy to carry. It isn't just about managing emotions. It's about embracing them. It's about finding freedom, growth, and the courage to live authentically in a world that often tells you to be anything but yourself. Recent research shows the toll that ignoring emotional health takes on individuals, especially young people. Depression, anxiety, loneliness, burnout—these aren't just statistics; they're silent battles fought daily by millions. Inside, you'll find tools, exercises, and real-life strategies to help you navigate life's emotional terrain. These aren't just concepts; they're pathways to reclaiming your strength, finding your voice, and standing in your power.

Listen: I Believe in You

I've been on this journey, too. And let me tell you: Is it easy? No. Is it challenging? Absolutely. But it's also transformational.

So here's my promise to you:

If you're breathing, it's not too late.

Not too late to rewrite your story. Not too late to find peace. Not too late to live a life that feels true to who you are.

Let's get started

"Your story isn't over until you say it is.
As long as you're breathing, transformation is possible.
The journey will shake you, but it's the quake that
builds your freedom." - Rasesha Rabari

"You Matter" Not because of what you do for others, not because of your accomplishments, not because of the roles you play in someone else's story—but simply because you exist. Your essence, your presence, your story—it all matters deeply. But understanding this is only the beginning. To truly embrace your worth, you must be willing to embark on a journey that demands honesty, courage, and evolution.

This journey isn't for everyone. It's not for those who find comfort in complaining or who thrive on blaming others for their circumstances. It's not for those who shy away from hard truths. No, this is a path for those who demand better—for themselves, from themselves—and who are willing to do the work.

Being the upgraded version of you doesn't mean you are perfect. It means willingness. An openness to see yourself beyond layers of conditioning, pain, and societal structures. It's about changing—not to be in line with someone else's ideals, but to be in alignment with your truth.

Seeing yourself the way you actually are requires uncompromised non-partial practice. It's not about feeling sorry for yourself or mollifying yourself through the waves of hardship you've experienced. It's about taking ownership of your growth and advocating for it. The journey is not about making excuses or complaining about what someone did to you, I get that. What matters is what you're going to do next.

How you show up for yourself. How you own your own being.

The outside world will beat down the battles, and diversions on you. It will try to pull you out of you — your personality, your principles, your reality. But here's the kicker: whatever you consume is completely your choice. While such a reference point is deeper for purposeful people, shallow people go on shallow references only. So I'll leave you with this question: What are you doing for what matters to you? Don't tell me what others did to you. Don't recount the times you were hurt or wronged. My interest isn't in them—it's in you. What decisions are you making? What beliefs guide you? What steps are you taking toward your freedom and growth? This is where your power lies.

Adopt this mantra: **"Witness, Don't Assume."**

"I trust you, but I believe what I witness and experience in your character." What does this mean? It's about aligning trust with evidence. If someone's actions match their words, they earn your trust. If they don't, you adjust your expectations—not out of bitterness, but out of wisdom.

This practice isn't cold or calculating; it's self-respect in action. It allows you to remain open-hearted without being naïve.

When you trust boundaries, you're not clinging to people who drain you. Self-love isn't about bubble baths and affirmations alone. It's about making choices that honor your values and protect your peace. Self-respect is the backbone of this love—it ensures that your actions align with your worth. Together, they create a powerful, resilient you.

> *"Boundaries are the love language you speak to yourself. When you honor them, you tell the world exactly how you deserve to be treated." - Rasesha Rabari.*

Life throws stones at you. What will you do—let them crush you or use them to build your empire? True strength is not in retaliation; it's in creation. Revenge is fleeting, but building something greater than your pain is eternal. That's where emotional health begins—not in reacting to life's chaos but in rising above it, crafting a reality that reflects your values, vision, and power.

Your Evolution Starts Within. The strongest bridge between self and service is built on two pillars:

1. **How you treat yourself**. Your boundaries, your self-talk, and your daily habits are the foundation of your inner empire.

2. **How you show up in the world**. Your relationships, your purpose, and your energy are reflections of that foundation.

Ancient yoga philosophy speaks of Yama (restraints) and Niyama (observances)—a timeless framework for self-mastery. The first step to emotional health is honoring yourself. Only then can you extend that honor outward.

It takes courage to be yourself in a world constantly telling you that you're not enough. But let me tell you something powerful: you are enough. The version of you that wakes up with doubts, wrestles with fears, and carries the weight of past pain—yes, even that version of you—is worthy of love and respect.

Loving yourself isn't just a self-help mantra; it's an act of reclaiming your power. It's choosing to hear what your pain is trying to teach you instead of begging for it to disappear. It's understanding that the story written so far doesn't define the rest of your journey. The pages ahead are yours to fill.

No one is coming to save you. No one will hand you your dreams on a silver platter. But that's a gift, not a curse. Because it means the power to change your life has been in your hands all along.

The problem with love in today's world is that we've been taught to see people through our eyes instead of our souls. Real love—whether for yourself or others—isn't about perfection. It's about connection, intention, and authenticity.

Let me ask you this: Are you waiting for someone to complete you? To validate your worth? To fill the gaps in your life? If so, you're missing the point. You have to love yourself so deeply that any love you receive from others simply adds to the abundance you've already created within.

You can't outsource your happiness. You can't delegate your worth.

You must be fearless enough to give yourself the love you didn't receive. When you know your worth, you stop settling for less. Strong people are single not because they're unlovable, but because they know what they bring to the table. It takes a higher level of authenticity, authority, and accountability to match their character.

They don't bend to societal expectations—they rise above them. Think of the story of Bhagiratha bringing the Ganga to earth. It wasn't easy. It required Shiva's strength to channel her immense power. Similarly, your character—your essence—demands a vessel strong enough to honor it. This is why you can't settle for shallow connections or empty promises.

Rights aren't rights if they can be taken away from you by someone. They're privileges. And in a conscious society, no one would need to fight for their rights because everyone would fulfill their duties. But we don't live in that world, which is why you must stand firm in your values and protect what matters.

So, let's stop trying to solve your entire life in one breath. Focus on adding one good thing at a time. Let your pile of good things grow. Appreciate who you are now while working toward the person you want to become. Relax and trust the timing of your life. You'll figure out your career. You'll find the right relationship. You'll become everything you're meant to be.

But don't forget: who you are today is already enough.

What if I told you that everything you've ever desired—success, love, connection, purpose—is already within reach? Yes, waiting for you. But here's the truth: it won't come knocking on your door. No dreams manifest themselves in silence; no blessings arrive without invitation. To summon them, you must take the first step.

Prayers are answered, blessings arrive, and intuition guides us because of one principle: energy responds to action. When you rise for yourself, when you dare to show up fully, the universe notices. Your courage becomes the signal—a declaration that you're ready to receive what you desire.

A Clean Slate for Growth

My Nanaji often said, "A good learner begins with a clean slate." Think about that. Can you write a new chapter on a messy blackboard? Can you sketch your dreams on a crumpled page? No. To create something meaningful, you must first declutter—your beliefs, your doubts, your fears. Unlearn what no longer serves you so you can make room for what will.

Your mindset works the same way. Old narratives of failure, inadequacy, or fear of judgment? They're outdated. Lets Erase Them. Replace them with the belief that you are enough, that you are capable, and that every small step propels you forward. This isn't an act of forgetting but of releasing.

Hey, let's get to the point: Your life, your happiness, your power—they all boil down to one simple truth: **Your Essence x Your Presence = Your Power**. Inside you is a universe of emotions, beliefs, and untapped potential, radiating out into everything you do. When you truly own your worth, everything shifts. You don't just exist—you **thrive**.

The Three Pillars of Self-Discovery This book is your guide through the three essential phases of life. **Each one builds on the other to unlock your full potential**: Together, these define who you are, how you show up in the world, and what you're capable of achieving. Let's explore how they interconnect and why mastering them is the key to emotional freedom. So, You Ready ..?

The Three Phases of Your Emotional Self -Discovery:

- **Your Essence: The Seed (LEARN):** This is where it all begins—deep within.

- **Your Presence: The Growth (EARN)**: Here's where you take what you've learned and bring it to life.

- **Your Power: The Bloom (RETURN)**: This is where everything comes together.

Your Essence: Owning Your Truth

Imagine this: You're the architect of your life. Your essence—your core—is the blueprint. But here's the twist: most people live their lives following someone else's design. Society tells you who to be, how to live, and what to chase. And you? You fall into the trap of proving yourself to a world that barely knows you.

Stop. Just stop. Your essence is not up for negotiation.

Your essence is the raw, unfiltered truth of who you are when no one is watching. It's the foundation of your values, your dreams, and your purpose.

Ask yourself:
- Who am I when I strip away fear, judgment, and doubt?

- What lights my soul on fire?

- Am I living my truth, or am I dimming my light to fit in?

- Who do I believe I am?

- Who do I want to become?

- What's my definition of success, happiness, and grace?

Through Your Essence, You Learn:
Self-exploration begins by understanding who you are. Your unique essence is the foundation of your growth—the curiosity that fuels knowledge and the courage to uncover your truth.

Knowing your essence and living your essence are two different things.
Most people know who they are but lack the courage to live as that person.

Why? Because it's messy. It's uncomfortable. But let me tell you this—it's worth it.

Ask yourself : Your Willingness to Take the Step On a scale of 1-10:

How willing are you to take one step today toward living authentically?

What's the one thing holding you back? Write it down. Face it. Name it.

Remember, the first step doesn't have to be grand—it just has to be yours.

Your Presence: Claiming Your Space

Let's talk about presence. It's not about how loud you are or how much attention you grab. Presence is energy—it's the way you make people feel, the way you show up, and the way you carry your essence into the world.

When your essence aligns with your presence, you become unstoppable. But misalignment? That's where chaos lives. You can't project confidence if you're drowning in self-doubt. You can't demand respect if you don't respect yourself. And you can't inspire others if you've abandoned your own dreams.

So, here's the deal: Your presence is your responsibility.

Ask yourself:
- Do I show up fully, or do I hold back out of fear?
- Is my energy a reflection of my true self, or am I faking it?
- Am I creating an environment where I thrive, or am I settling?

Does Your Intention Have Your Attention? Think of one goal you're passionate about.

Now ask:
- Am I giving it my full attention, or am I distracted by fear, procrastination, or doubt?
- What's one action I can take today to align my attention with my intention?

Through Your Presence, You Earn:
Your presence is your gift to the world. By showing up authentically and fully engaged, you create opportunities to build relationships, wealth, and wisdom. What you earn is a reflection of the energy you share.

Your Power: Transforming Potential Into Impact

Power isn't about controlling others—it's about owning yourself. It's the ability to stand tall in your truth, even when the world tries to shake you. But let me make this clear: Power isn't given; it's claimed.

True power is quiet, focused, and relentless.

It's the ability to:
- Set boundaries without guilt.
- Forgive without forgetting your worth.
- Walk away from what no longer serves you—not with anger, but with grace.

Think about this: When you know your essence and show up fully in your presence, you become magnetic. You stop chasing and start attracting. You stop proving and start embodying. That's power.

Through Your Power, You Return:
True fulfillment comes when you harness your power to give back. Returning to the universe means using your success to uplift others, heal wounds, and leave behind a legacy of love and purpose.

Here's a hard truth: The story you're living today is the story you've accepted. If it's not serving you, rewrite it. Take a clean slate, erase the doubts, and start over. The beauty of life is that it's never too late to change the plot.

Winning at Life—Redefined What does success mean to you? If your answer is money, fame, or validation, let's rethink that. True success is waking up every day knowing you're aligned with your essence. It's about growth, fulfillment, and impact.

Ask yourself:
- What would a successful life look like for me—not for society, not for my parents, but for me?

- What steps am I taking to create that life?

This entire process is a bridge. It's the journey from "becoming to achieve" to the paradox of "achieving to become." And those who understand this thin line difference are the ones who truly win at life.

I believe : You Are the Architect of Your Life:

- **You're the only one** who truly knows your worth.

- **You're the only one** who can take a stand for yourself.

- **You're the only one** who can decide to bring change to your life.

- **You're the only one** who can silence the noise of doubt and listen to your inner voice.

- **You're the only one** who can prove yourself right—or wrong.

So, from this very moment let's start looking at ourselves;

1. **Smile at yourself every time you see your reflection.** Celebrate the person staring back at you. You've come further than you think.

2. **Wink at yourself when you achieve something, big or small.** Let your inner voice say, "You're amazing, and you've got this."

3. **Wear what makes you feel powerful.** Stop dressing to impress others. Dress to feel unstoppable.

These aren't just habits—they're declarations. They're acts of self-love and empowerment.

Listen closely. You are enough. You've always been enough. Stop waiting for someone to validate you. Stop believing the lie that you need to become someone else. You don't need a makeover. You need to uncover the masterpiece you already are.

And let me tell you something: The road to your power? It's not smooth, and it's not easy. It's going to challenge you. You're going to cry. You're going to face fears that shake you. But every tear, every moment of doubt, every step forward—it's worth it.

This isn't motivational fluff. This is your wake-up call. Stop shrinking. Stop doubting. It's time to rise. Because **"YOU MATTER"**. **Your dreams matter.** And the world is waiting for **"YOU"** to show up and shine.

Are you ready? Let's do this.

— Your guide on this journey, I am Rasesha Rabari who believes in YOU.

Let me share how this realization hit me like a thunderbolt.

I was in Goa, immersed in my 500-hour yoga teacher training course. I had enrolled not just to deepen my practice but to reconnect with myself. I was tired of running on autopilot and ignoring the whispers of my soul. My Guruji Yog Namito, introduced me to the story of Rabiya al-Adabiya during one of our philosophy sessions.

Rabiya's Wisdom: Finding the Light Within

One evening, as the fiery glow of the setting sun bathed the village streets, Rabiya al-Adabiya, a woman known as much for her eccentricity as for her profound wisdom, stood bent over, searching for something on the dusty road. She was old, her frail body moving slowly, but her eyes carried an intensity that defied her age.

A young traveler passing through the village noticed her and stopped out of concern. He had no idea who she was, only that she seemed troubled. "Excuse me, Ma'am," he said, his voice laced with genuine care, "What are you looking for? It's almost dark, and searching in this light must be difficult. Let me help you."

Rabiya looked up, her face lighting up with a warm smile. "Thank you, kind stranger," she said, her voice gentle but resolute. "You are the first to offer help. The people of this village think I've gone mad."

The man chuckled nervously. "Well, what have you lost? I'll help you find it."

"I've lost a needle," Rabiya said plainly, returning her focus to the ground.

The man frowned. "A needle? Out here on the road? It's so small, and the light is fading fast. Tell me, where exactly did it fall? Maybe we'll find it if we focus on the spot."

Rabiya hesitated, then laughed softly, a sound filled with both mischief and wisdom. "Ah, that's the tricky part. I didn't lose it out here. I lost it inside my house."

The man was stunned. "Inside your house? Then why are you searching for it out here?"

Rabiya nodded thoughtfully. "Because it's too dark inside my house. I don't have a lamp, and I thought it would be easier to search outside where there's still a little light."

The man stared at her in disbelief, shaking his head. "With all due respect, that's absurd. If you lost it inside, searching outside won't help, no matter how much light there is here."

Rabiya's eyes twinkled as she straightened herself, a subtle power radiating from her frail frame. "You're absolutely right," she said, her tone shifting to one of quiet authority. "But isn't this what everyone in the world is doing? They lose themselves, their treasures—peace, love, joy, and purpose—inside their hearts, yet they search for them outside because it seems easier. They look for happiness in possessions, love in validation, and peace in fleeting pleasures. The question is not where it's easier to search. The question is: where did you lose it?"

The young man was speechless. Her words pierced through him like arrows, striking the very core of his own struggles.

Rabiya continued, her voice growing more intense. "The truth is simple. We've all lost our treasures inside ourselves, but we're too afraid to search there because it feels dark and unfamiliar. Yes, the outside world is full of light and distraction, but it can't give us what we've lost within. And here's the irony: the darkness we fear inside is not an enemy. It holds the eternal light that needs no fuel, no sun, no flame. That light is your essence, your truth, your power."

Rabiya paused, her gaze steady. "So, my dear stranger, will you gather the courage to stop searching outside? Will you walk into your own darkness and find the light waiting for you? Because that is where the real journey begins."

The young man bowed his head, humbled by her wisdom. He knew her words were not just for him— they were for anyone willing to listen.

Conclusion: The Light Within

The story of Rabiya al-Adabiya is a powerful reminder that our essence—our deepest treasures—are not lost in the external world but hidden within ourselves. The search may feel daunting because it requires us to confront our fears, insecurities, and the unknown. Yet, this inner journey is the only path to true fulfillment.

The darkness inside is not the absence of light—it is the gateway to enlightenment. By owning our essence and facing what lies within, we unlock the eternal light of our true selves, a light that never dims and never depends on external fuel.

My take away:

When Guruji told the story, I felt it land deep in my heart. It was as if Rabiya's wisdom unlocked a part of me I had kept locked away. In her tale, I saw my own struggles—my search for validation, my habit of looking outside for answers I had lost within.

That story hit me hard. It shook me awake. I realized how often I had searched for joy, self-worth, and peace in external sources. I'd blame circumstances or other people when I felt lost or unloved. But Rabiya's words made me pause. They challenged me to face the truth: the light I sought wasn't out there. It had always been inside me. I just needed to stop running and turn inward.....!!

This story, my friend, was a turning point. It taught me to respect my struggles, to own my essence, and to take back my power. And today, I'm sharing it with you because I believe it can do the same for you.

Exercise: Finding Your Needle

- Sit in a quiet place with your eyes closed. Take three deep breaths.

- Ask yourself: What have I lost inside me? Write down your answers, no matter how simple or complicated.

- Now ask: Where am I searching for it? Reflect on whether your external search aligns with where you lost it.

- Commit to one small action that takes you inward—meditation, journaling, or simply sitting with your thoughts.

No matter where you are in life, no matter how lost you feel, I want you to know this: your answers are not out there. They are within. You don't need anyone's permission to believe in yourself. You don't need external light to guide your way. The light inside you is enough.

You matter. Your essence matters. And the first step to reclaiming your life is owning that truth. Your light is waiting—it's time to find it.

*"Your perspective isn't just how you
see life—it's how you shape it."*
– Rasesha Rabari

Your Essence

The Seed

"Life isn't about finding yourself in others; it's about creating yourself in the most unapologetic, authentic way possible. Your essence is your superpower—never trade it for approval." - Rasesha Rabari

The only direction from here is inwards, and the only obstacle is the comfort zone you've been living in. Everything you want, everything you've ever dreamed of, lies just beyond the boundary of what feels safe and familiar. But here's the truth: growth doesn't happen without trade-offs. Every step forward requires leaving something behind—fear, doubt, excuses, or even old versions of yourself.

What I've learned from my journey is this: the higher you climb, the greater the price. You can't ascend to the next level by simply wishing for it or taking half-hearted steps. No, true progress demands a willingness to let go, to sacrifice what's comfortable for what's possible.

To rise to the next level in life, you must respect yourself first. Why? Because the respect you seek from others can never satisfy you if you don't honor your own worth. When you truly know your value, the world will see it too.

You don't control everything. You can't control how fast the seed grows, but you do control how much care and effort you give it. Your focus must always be on giving your 100%—on showing up, doing the work, and trusting that the results will follow.

I invite you for a reality check: letting go of old beliefs, the excuses, the victimisation standing upright to face and accept our own reality.

Here's the truth: the only way to lose is to give up on yourself. If you show up, day after day—no matter how hard it gets—the victory is already yours. This isn't just about overcoming obstacles. It's about breaking free from the emotional baggage holding you back—the fear, doubt, and past failures that no longer have a place in your future.

Growth demands a trade-off. You'll have to let go of the old to make room for the new. That might mean releasing outdated habits, cutting ties with toxic relationships, or letting go of beliefs that no longer serve you.

But here's the power: each time you release what weighs you down, you move closer to the life you deserve. Growth isn't easy, but it's worth it. The higher you climb, the more rewarding the view becomes. So rise—this is your time.

Let's get real—nobody's life is perfect. Not yours, not mine, not the person you admire on social media. The illusion of perfection is just that: an illusion. Behind the smiles, the filtered photos, and the curated success stories, there are battles being fought in silence.

Think about it: the person in that luxury car might be battling loneliness. The couple showing off their "perfect" relationship might be barely speaking at home. Would you truly trade your struggles for theirs? Probably not. Because life isn't about chasing perfection—it's about embracing authenticity.

Stop comparing your behind-the-scenes mess to someone else's highlight reel. Your worth isn't found in how flawless your life looks but in the raw, unfiltered, and beautiful journey you're on. The truth is, your struggles don't define you—they shape you, prepare you, and strengthen you for the greatness that lies ahead.

Everything you want lies just outside your comfort zone. But here's the hard truth: to reach it, you'll have to make trade-offs. You can't rise to the next level in life by staying where you are. Growth demands sacrifice—the kind of sacrifice that requires courage, consistency, and a commitment to evolution.

At every stage of your journey, you'll face decisions that challenge you. **Do you cling to what's familiar**, or do you step into the unknown? The higher you aim, the greater the price you must pay. It's not just about effort; it's about letting go of what no longer serves you—doubt, fear, excuses—and stepping fully into your potential.

Your past victories? They're meaningful, but they're not enough. Growth isn't a one-time event; it's a lifelong process. The steps you took yesterday were important, but What truly matters is what you do now. Consistency isn't optional; it's your proof that you believe in yourself. The moment you stop evolving, you stop living. Stagnation is like still water—it attracts decay. The same is true for your mindset. Keep moving, keep growing, or risk losing the sharpness of your thoughts and the intensity of your dreams.

The Tale of Two Siblings: A Lesson in Patience

Imagine two siblings entrusted with a simple task: planting a seed in their grandmother's garden. Both were given the same instructions—plant the seed, water it daily, and let time do its magic. The elder sibling, brimming with curiosity and impatience, couldn't resist the urge to check the seed's progress. Every morning, they dug up the soil to see if it had sprouted, disrupting its fragile beginnings. Despite their grandmother's gentle reminders that growth happens underground, invisible to the eye, they couldn't wait.

The younger sibling, however, chose a different path. They planted the seed and trusted the process. Day by day, they watered the soil, whispered words of encouragement to the earth, and let nature take its course. It wasn't always easy; doubt and impatience crept in at times, but they remembered their grandmother's wisdom: "Growth happens in the unseen moments."

Days turned into weeks. The elder sibling's seed never sprouted. The constant interference had damaged its delicate roots, robbing it of its potential. Meanwhile, the younger sibling's seed broke through the soil one morning, revealing its first green shoot. Over time, that tiny sprout blossomed into a vibrant plant, its fragrance filling the garden.

Emotional Impatience: A Hidden Saboteur

This story isn't just about planting seeds—it's about how we navigate life. The elder sibling's impatience mirrors how many of us approach our dreams, relationships, or personal growth. We crave immediate results, and when we don't see progress, we panic, meddle, or even abandon the process entirely.

But life operates on its own timeline. True growth—the kind that transforms you—happens in the quiet, unseen moments. It's in the disciplined efforts you repeat daily, even when there's no visible outcome. Like the younger sibling, you must nurture your goals with trust, patience, and unwavering belief.

Conclusion:

Impatience is rooted in fear—the fear that what we're working toward might not happen. But impatience doesn't speed things up; it derails the process. Imagine if every caterpillar abandoned its cocoon because it couldn't see its wings yet. Transformation takes time.

Instead of fixating on the outcome, shift your focus to the process. Water your dreams. Feed your ambitions. Let the roots take hold beneath the surface. The growth may be invisible for a while, but when it breaks through, the results will speak for themselves.

*"Your life blossoms not because you rush it,
but because you trust it. Growth is a process,
not a performance. Honor it, and soon enough,
you'll see the fruits of your patience."*
- Rasesha Rabari

Focus on What Can Be Done

Regret is a silent thief. It sneaks into your mind, "what-ifs," draining your energy and chaining you to the past. But here's the truth: regret only holds power if you give it permission. Yesterday is done. It's unchangeable. What you can change is the way you show up today.

Every moment spent dwelling on what went wrong is a missed opportunity to create something right. Progress doesn't demand perfection—it demands a decision. A single action. No matter how small, forward movement is what builds momentum. Shift Your Focus to Possibility Instead of asking, "Why did this happen to me?" ask, "What can I do with it now?" That one shift transforms your energy from helplessness to empowerment. Whether it's starting fresh, forgiving yourself, or pursuing a long-lost dream, the key is in taking action.

Embrace Your Humanity
Here's the deal: nobody raises their standards without stumbling. I've made my share of mistakes—big ones.

But you know what? Shame, failure, judgment, and regret aren't barriers; they're stepping stones. They shape you into someone stronger, wiser, and more capable. Crying over a misstep is human, but staying stuck in that emotion is a choice. Don't let regret control your life. Let it teach you. Every stumble is a lesson; every lesson is a step toward something greater.

Honing Your Internal Compass

Your Glass Isn't Empty:

Let me remind you of life-changing news: your glass is not empty. Sure, sometimes, it feels half-empty, but here's the reality — it's half-full, too. And even better? It's refillable. You have the power to decide what to pour into it.

You can focus on what's absent or accept responsibility and pour into your vessel what you need to create the life you want." Yes, life's challenges can make us take for granted what we already have, but here's a question for you: what if the life you're living right now is the same life someone else is praying for? Think about it.

We're so caught up in chasing the next big thing that we stop appreciating what we've already achieved.

Tony Robbins said it best: "Humans are born crying, live complaining, and die unsatisfied."

If something feels missing, don't just cry over it—refill, recreate, replace. Your glass is your chance to realign, rebuild, and reimagine your life. It's a blessing in disguise, a gift waiting for you to unwrap.

Now, let's talk about risk. What's the greater risk in life? 1) Never taking a chance, stuck in fear of failure or judgment. OR 2) Taking a shot at growth where there's at least a possibility of things getting better? The answer is obvious.

The glass isn't just half-empty—it's your opportunity to fill it with your dreams, your goals, and the wishlist you left behind in the race to be "perfect." Choose wisely.

Ask yourself:

What's your biggest dream that's still on your wishlist?

Are you focusing on your blessings or your gaps?

What's one risk you've been avoiding that could lead to growth?

Your glass is waiting. How will you fill it?

Until & unless they hold your hand and address you directly with what they have to say, don't take anything personally. People gossip talk indirectly because they have the courage to say it on your face, they also know that what they are spreading is just something created to satisfy their need to talk about you - because all that they can do is just that - only that is in their control. To become anything near to who you are is a distant future to them. Not all have the courage & capacity of hard work.

Here's a game-changing truth: most of what people say or do isn't about you—it's about them. Their words and actions are reflections of their own struggles, fears, and insecurities.

The moment you stop taking things personally, you take your power back. You free yourself from the need for external validation and step fully into your own worth.

In a world that profits from your self-doubt, choosing to like yourself is a radical act. It's liberating and transformative. The moment you stop letting others dictate your value, you gain clarity, peace, and confidence.

Myths You Need to Disown:

Myth: "I need others to believe in me to succeed."

Truth: The only belief that matters is your own.

Myth: "If I fail, I'm not good enough."

Truth: Failure is a stepping stone, not a judgment of your worth.

Myth: "I'll never be ready."

Truth: You're ready the moment you decide to act.

Your Essence guides your choices

Every decision we make shapes our future, one step at a time. Each choice—big or small—creates ripple effects that define who we are and what our lives become. But if this is true, why do so many of us repeatedly make decisions that don't serve us? The answer lies not in luck or logic, but in understanding what truly drives our decisions.

The secret to mastering decision-making is simple yet profound: learn to harness pain and pleasure, rather than letting them control you. Most people are driven by the need to avoid pain more than the desire to experience pleasure, often without realizing it. This subconscious mechanism guides everything we do. Yet, when we take control of this dynamic, we reclaim the power to shape our lives with intention.

The Lens That Shapes Your Reality

What you focus on becomes your reality. Your mind is like a camera, zooming in on certain aspects of life while blurring out others. Where you direct your attention defines how you feel—and those feelings, in turn, dictate your actions.

Think about this: Do you concentrate on what you can control or what is no longer in your hands? Are you stuck in the past, ruminating about the present or dreaming a desired future into existence? What we focus on; therefore, defines how we feel and the decisions we make.

You are responding, on an unconscious level, every moment of your life, three fundamental queries:

- What will I focus on?

- Will it be fear, resentment or past failures? Or will it be hope, gratitude and possibility?

- What does this mean to me? A challenge or an opportunity? A punishment or a gift?

Your actions are based on the meaning you give to an experience.

The process of better decision-making starts with shifting your brain from focusing on the unchangeable to the controllable. Let go of the past, and choose to stay present now, building an amazing future.

Nurturing a Growth-Oriented Mindset

The Quiet Code Of Your Choice

Your standards set the boundaries for your life. They are the invisible lines that define what you'll accept, how you behave, and the quality of your decisions. Unlike self-control, which can be depleted, your standards act as a consistent guide.

High standards push you to make better choices, while low standards allow mediocrity to creep in. When faced with a decision—whether it's resisting temptation, taking action, or holding back—the outcome depends on the expectations you set for yourself.

It's not about perfection, it's about progress. It's deciding that you refuse to settle for less than what you're capable of. If you hold your standards in alignment with your values and the goals you aspire to achieve, your decisions automatically rise to meet them.

The Fire That Fuels Success:

True achievers aren't driven by luck or talent—they're propelled by an insatiable hunger for growth and success. This inner drive isn't about avoiding failure but using it as fuel to push forward.

Hunger isn't about willpower; it's about standards. People with relentless hunger raise their standards, push through adversity, and learn from setbacks rather than letting them define them. They understand that failure isn't a dead end—it's a stepping stone.

The best part? Hunger can be cultivated. Surround yourself with people who challenge and inspire you. Seek out goals that ignite your passion. Choose beliefs that empower you. Hunger grows with every decision you make to move closer to your potential.

The Promise of Character (Story)

There are moments in life that don't just stay with you—they transform you. They shape the essence of who you are and the person you strive to become. One such moment for me took place during my school days, on a journey that was meant to be routine but ended up becoming a defining chapter of my life.

As a curious and ambitious 14-year-old, I looked up to my father, Mr. V. V. Rabari. To the world, he was a man of stature, discipline, and achievement—a figure many aspired to emulate. But to me, he was much more: he was the embodiment of integrity, wisdom, and unwavering values. Every interaction with him felt like a masterclass in life, and I wanted nothing more than to learn from him and, someday, walk in his footsteps.

The Climb to Chotila

Our trips to Chotila, a revered temple perched atop a hill 200 kilometers from Ahmedabad, were a ritual we shared. It was one of the few times I got my father's undivided attention, and I cherished every second of it. The temple was accessible by a steep climb of 700 steps—a test of both physical endurance and mental resilience.

On this particular visit, I was bubbling with energy as we started the ascent. My head was filled with excitement, eager to share with him what I had recently learned in school about gravitational force. But as the climb grew steeper, my enthusiasm waned. My legs burned, my breath quickened, and my words faded into silence.

My father, on the other hand, moved steadily, unshaken by the effort. His calm pace and unwavering focus stood in stark contrast to my struggle. When we finally reached the temple, I was both relieved and exhausted. After offering our prayers, we began the descent, and that's when a question took root in my mind.

The Question That Changed Everything

As we descended the steps, I turned to my father and asked, "Dad, why is it so much easier to climb down than to climb up? Is it because of gravity?"

I expected a scientific explanation. What I got instead was a lesson that would stay with me for the rest of my life.

He paused, looked at me with his wise, steady eyes, and said, "It's easy to drop down in life, my child. To lower your standards, to let go of your values, to lose control over your words or actions—it takes no effort at all. But to climb up, to elevate yourself, to live with dignity and purpose, now that requires real strength. That's the difference. Falling is effortless, but rising takes character and courage."

His words struck me deeply. It wasn't just advice; it was a mirror reflecting the choices we all face every day. My father placed his hand gently on my head and added, "This is what I want you to remember: it's easy to lose yourself in this world—to let go of what makes you, *you*. But protecting your values, your kindness, your integrity—that's what defines you. That's what makes you strong."

The Power of a Promise

I couldn't help but ask, "But Dad, how do you stay strong? How do you live with confidence and protect your values?"

He smiled and replied, "By making a promise to yourself—a promise you never break. My promise is simple: I will never let anyone or anything make me bitter. No matter what happens, I have vowed to live a life of grace."

Those words held a power I couldn't fully grasp at the time, but I knew they were important. He continued, "The moment you allow someone else's actions to make you bitter, you lose control of yourself. You let the world dictate who you are. But if you protect your values, they will protect you. Your confidence isn't found in what others think of you; it's in the promises you keep to yourself."

Right there, on those ancient stone steps, I made my own promise. I promised to live by the values he had taught me: strength, kindness, integrity, and grace.

The Legacy of Values

That day wasn't just another visit to Chotila; it was the moment I chose who I wanted to be. My father didn't just give me advice—he gave me a foundation to build my life upon.

Over the years, life has tested me. There have been moments when it felt easier to give into bitterness, to let go of the values that require so much effort to uphold. But every time I'm tempted, I think of my father's quiet strength. I think of the promise he made to himself and the promise I made to myself.

Those values have become my compass, guiding me through challenges and anchoring me in moments of doubt. They remind me that rising isn't about perfection; it's about persistence. It's about choosing grace when the world gives you every reason to be bitter.

What Defines You

Life will always test your character. It will tempt you to take the easy way out, to abandon your principles, to let the actions of others dictate your emotions. But the true measure of a person is not in how they fall—it's in how they rise.

Your confidence doesn't come from external validation. It comes from the promises you make to yourself and the courage to honor them. It comes from knowing that no matter how hard the climb, you're choosing to elevate yourself.

Your Turn: Define Your Promise

Exercise:

Take a moment to reflect on your values and write down the following:

1. **One value** you refuse to compromise, no matter the circumstance.

2. **One action** you can take today to protect that value.

3. **One promise** you can make to yourself to live with confidence and grace.

Conclusion:

The same boiling water softens a potato and hardens an egg. The circumstances you face don't define you—your response to them does. Life will test your patience, your strength, and your values. But the choice to rise, to stay true to yourself, and to live with grace is always yours.

You can't change the world by complaining about it. But you can inspire change by living your values. Stop waiting for life to be easy—it never promised to be. Instead, make a promise to yourself: You will rise. You will protect your essence. You will live with courage and character.

The world doesn't need perfect people; it needs people who choose to rise above. Be one of them.

Let's face it—expressing emotions can feel risky. Society teaches us that vulnerability equals weakness. Maybe you've been judged, betrayed, or dismissed when you opened up. Those experiences sting, and it's easy to conclude that suppressing emotions is the safest route. But here's the truth: the problem isn't that you expressed yourself; it's that you shared with the wrong people.

Not everyone deserves access to your inner world. Trusting the wrong individuals can lead to leaks, gossip, and pain. But instead of shutting down and punishing yourself, it's time to get intentional about your circle. Surround yourself with people who uplift you, value your emotions, and truly want to see you thrive. Finding those people won't happen overnight, but they're worth the effort.

Here's a vital mindset shift: **you can't punish yourself for what others have done to you**. It's not about cutting off your ability to feel or share; it's about sharpening your ability to choose. Think of it this way: if a nail breaks, you don't stop using your finger—you learn how to care for it better.

Upgrading your circle is the key. Hanging out with people less evolved than you might feel comfortable because they make you feel superior. But comfort doesn't equal growth. True progress happens when you surround yourself with people who challenge you intellectually and emotionally—people who inspire your evolution.

So, ask yourself:

1. Do you feel safe expressing your emotions with your current circle?

2. How often do you find yourself suppressing emotions out of fear of judgment?

3. Are you actively seeking relationships that align with your growth and values?

The right connections don't just make you feel heard—they elevate you. Choose wisely, and don't settle for less than you deserve.

Building Foundations for Success and Connection

Belonging to Yourself:

Belonging to yourself is the most authentic and transformative journey you will ever undertake. It demands that you strip away societal masks and stand firm in your truth. Yet, within this sacred discomfort lies the magic of discovering your essence.

True belonging isn't about being accepted by others; it's about accepting yourself. It's the power of choosing your authenticity over conformity, even when it feels risky. What's riskier—losing yourself to fit in or losing others to remain authentic? The answer is clear: betraying your essence is the greatest loss of all.

The truth is, we're often unkind to ourselves. We silence our emotions, fearing judgment. But what you feel is valuable; it shapes your decisions, your growth, and your future. Let's debunk some myths about vulnerability and independence that hold us back from true belonging.

Myth #1:

We've been conditioned to think vulnerability equals weakness, but it's the opposite. Vulnerability is the birthplace of courage. Every bold act you've ever admired requires someone to step into uncertainty, risk, and emotional exposure. Neuroscience backs this up: vulnerability activates the same regions in the brain that foster connection, trust, and empathy.

As children, we believed adulthood would make us invincible, that we'd outgrow vulnerability. The truth? To grow is to embrace it. Vulnerability isn't something to outgrow; it's the strength that allows us to love, connect, and thrive.

Myth #2:

Our society romanticizes rugged individualism, but the reality is, we were never designed to walk alone. Neuroscience reveals that our greatest strength comes not from isolation but from collaboration. To grow as humans is to become dependable and interdependent. Our resilience and success are rooted in our ability to connect, plan, and work with others.

Choosing vulnerability doesn't mean sharing everything with everyone. It means finding the right people—the ones who cherish your essence and support your growth. The wrong ones will exploit your openness; the right ones will treasure it and protect your trust.

The Courage to Confront Your Truth:

In your journey toward belonging, you must confront your truth. You can't numb it, escape it, or ignore it. The stories you carry—both the triumphs and the struggles—shape your identity. But they don't dictate your future unless you let them.

To rise, you must face your shadows. Own your story, not to erase it, but to rewrite its ending. Growth doesn't mean dismissing your pain; it means integrating it into your wholeness. Vulnerability isn't the obstacle—it's the gateway to your greatest light.

Choosing the Right Circle:

Your growth depends on the people you surround yourself with. Hanging around those less evolved might make you feel superior, but it will never challenge you to grow. Surrounding yourself with more evolved, thoughtful, and supportive individuals ensures that your journey is forward-focused.

Find the people who make you feel seen and heard. Build relationships where you can discuss, not suppress, your dreams and fears. The right connections don't just support you—they elevate you.

Hey , Listen up because I'm talking directly to YOU. Here's a truth you might not want to hear: **stepping into vulnerability is one of the bravest things you'll ever do**. I know what you've been told. Vulnerability? It's a weakness, right? It's giving people the ammunition to hurt you. But let me flip that script for you: vulnerability isn't weakness. It's raw power.

When you try to strip uncertainty, risk, and emotional exposure out of your relationships—guess what? You rob courage of its oxygen. You're playing small. You're building walls, not connections. And deep down, you know that's not the life you want.

Here's the catch: not everyone deserves access to the real you. Yes, there are people who will exploit your openness—but here's the magic: the RIGHT people will honor it. They'll handle your truth with care— not because they have to, but because they want to. They'll see your courage for what it is: a gift.

So trust yourself. You're smarter than you think, and you already know who's worthy of your heart and who isn't. Stop wasting energy on proving yourself to people who will never get it.

When you embrace your authentic self—vulnerabilities, quirks, scars, and all—and stand rooted in your values, you don't just live a life. You design one. A life that's vibrant, full of purpose, and entirely yours.

And let me tell you something else: don't fear the wilderness of self-discovery. That wild, messy journey? It's where you find YOU. Your real belonging isn't about fitting in. It's about standing out in your truth.

So go ahead, step into that space of uncertainty. Be tender. Be brave. Be YOU.

I believe in you. Now it's time for you to believe it too.

— I am your guide and biggest fan on this journey.

Where Do You Stand with Vulnerability?

1. When faced with uncertainty, do you lean into it or avoid it at all costs?

    - I lean in and embrace the challenge.

    - I avoid it and hope it resolves itself.

    - It depends on the situation.

2. Do you believe asking for help is a sign of strength or weakness?

    - It's a sign of strength.

    - It feels like weakness to me.

    - I'm not sure—I struggle with this.

3. How often do you find yourself afraid to share your true thoughts or feelings?

   - Frequently—I worry about judgment.

   - Rarely—I'm comfortable being honest.

   - Sometimes—it depends on the context.

4. Do you feel that vulnerability helps or hinders relationships?

   - It helps deepen them.

   - It hinders—it feels risky.

   - I'm not sure—it's complicated.

5. Are you comfortable setting boundaries when sharing personal experiences?

   - Yes—I know what's okay and what's not.

   - No—I feel guilty setting limits.

   - Sometimes—it's situational.

Designing a Life Aligned with Your Values

Let's Change The Narrative:

Pause for a moment. Close your eyes and ask yourself:

- *How does my life truly look right now?*

- *How do I feel about who I am?*

Here's the truth: The voice you carry in your mind is either your greatest ally or your worst enemy. If your self-talk is clear, confident, and rooted in belief, your life will reflect that. If it's clouded with doubt, fear, and insecurity, so will your outcomes.

Let's simplify this: **The stronger you believe in your own worth, the more success you will create.** When your self-talk is filled with conviction, you don't merely navigate life—you dominate it. You rise above the noise and take full control of your narrative.

But if your thoughts are filled with doubt and constant second-guessing, you will find yourself trapped in a cycle of unrealized potential.

Lord Krishna said something profound that I want you to really hear: *"The one who cannot see himself, expects others to see him, to validate him. But the truth is, others are unaware of your expectations. They are trapped in their own self-doubt, their own insecurities. How can someone who doesn't know themselves truly see or validate you?"*

What does this mean? It means that if you don't know your own value, **how can you expect anyone else to see it?** You're seeking validation from people who are just as lost in their own struggles. They can't reflect back to you what you fail to see in yourself. **Stop waiting for others to validate you. Start validating yourself.** Own your worth, get crystal clear on your values, and **live by them unapologetically.**

Time for Value Addition

Do you want to earn respect & success both.? Here's the golden rule: **"Do what you said you will do."** In a world where trust is often broken, where people and circumstances fall short, the only person you can always rely on is **you**. Be the change you seek. Live by your word, and let your actions speak louder than any external noise.

The rejection, the failures, the heartaches you've endured—they've scarred your self-talk. I get it. But let's shift the narrative around rejection.

Ever seen a rocket launch? It's an incredible sight. The rocket ascends into the sky, and as it reaches a certain height, the boosters detach. Why? Not because the boosters don't understand the value of the rocket. But because the rocket has outgrown them. The boosters have served their purpose, but now, they would only hold the rocket back. **This is how growth works.** As you evolve, people, situations, and even beliefs that once served you will no longer align. **You will outgrow them.** They can't keep up with your evolution, and they no longer know your worth. That's when you must detach and move forward.

Evolution is the key. Constantly working on yourself. Striving for growth. The moment you stop evolving, you begin to stagnate. And stagnation? **That's where dreams die.** But let's be clear—letting go is not giving up. Letting go is giving space to grow. **If things are meant to work out, they will, in their own time**. And sometimes, that means stepping away for a moment. Let the situation breathe. Let the space between allow both parties to evolve. Reconnection, when it's right, will come. Relationships can be redefined, but only after growth has taken place.

Financial Freedom:
A Non-Negotiable Right

Stop daydreaming about financial freedom while doing nothing to create it. Desire alone won't pay the bills or fund your dreams. It's the **hunger** to go higher, paired with relentless dedication and unshakable discipline, that turns goals into reality.

Think about it: when you're financially dependent, you're living in survival mode. You don't have the freedom to make choices aligned with your values, passions, or purpose. You're stuck in a cycle where your dreams are sidelined because your resources don't match your ambitions.

Freedom Requires Responsibility:

Let's break this down.

Responsibility = Response + Ability.

Your ability to respond to challenges directly influences your level of freedom. Want to demand a better life? Then you need to act. Learn to earn, manage, and grow your wealth. You can't demand empowerment without taking ownership of your financial reality.

And don't mistake me—this isn't about greed. It's about growth. Financial independence is the gateway to self-respect, confidence, and opportunity. It's about having the power to say "yes" to your dreams and "no" to anything that compromises them.

So, what's stopping you? Commit to stepping up. Learn the skills, build the discipline, and take the necessary risks. Because when you own your financial reality, you own your future.

Freedom isn't handed out—it's earned. And if you want to live a life that reflects your true potential, you must take charge of your financial journey. You don't just deserve financial freedom; it's your right. So, stop waiting. Start **doing.**

Your financial freedom is not optional. It's essential. When you're financially independent, you're no longer at the mercy of others. You stand on your own two feet. And let me be blunt: if you can't provide for your basic financial needs, it's time to change that. **This is non-negotiable**.

When you learn to manage your money, it gives you control over your destiny.

I'm here to tell you: it's time to change your narrative. The quality of your life is directly linked to the quality of your self-talk. **You are what you tell yourself you are.**

Don't wait for someone else to validate your worth. **Validate yourself.**

Let me give you some powerful truths:

1. **If you cannot trust yourself, your dreams, your words—why should anyone else?** No one is going

to resonate with a person who doesn't believe in themselves. **Trust yourself first.**

2. **If you want freedom with no responsibility,** understand this: there's only one person on Earth who gets that deal—**a baby.** Do you really want to fight for the right to be a baby, to avoid responsibility? **Grow up.** Take responsibility for your life.

3. **Rejection doesn't mean you're less.** It just means your values don't align at this moment. Letting go doesn't mean giving up. It means you're giving yourself, and others, the time and space to grow. If something is meant to work out, it will—after growth has happened. And sometimes, that growth requires distance. Relationships are not lost—they are **redefined.**

4. **The greatest relief you can feel** is knowing that you will never, ever have to ask for financial help for your basic needs. That's the power of self-sufficiency. **That's the power of freedom.**

I've walked this path and know the power of owning your life. Everything you desire is within reach—it starts with your decision to believe in yourself.

"The wilderness within you is not your battleground; it's the birthplace of your courage, your truth, and your infinite light."
— *Rasesha Rabari*

Your moment to take control.

This exercise will help you recognize where you are letting your boundaries be disrespected, improve your communication, and take actionable steps to overcome procrastination. It's time to stop playing small and start living large.

Step 1: Recognizing Boundary Violations

Identify Areas of Weak Boundaries

Take a few minutes and reflect on the situations where your boundaries are frequently violated. Are there specific people or situations that constantly challenge your limits? Write them down.

Examples:

- People overstay their welcome at your home.
- Friends or colleagues regularly ask for favors you don't feel comfortable giving.
- You say "yes" when you really mean "no."

Do any of these apply to you?:

- **You don't take yourself seriously:** Are you letting others walk all over you because you believe you don't deserve better?
- **You don't hold people accountable**: Do you let people slide when they disrespect your time or space?
- **You apologize for setting boundaries:** Do you feel guilty for saying "no"?

- **You allow too much flexibility**: Do you bend over backward to avoid confrontation or discomfort?

- **You speak in uncertain terms:** Do you hedge or qualify your needs with statements like, "I think I need some space"?

- **You haven't verbalized your boundaries**: Are your boundaries just thoughts in your head, not spoken out loud?

- **You assume once is enough**: Do you think stating your boundary once is sufficient, even when it's been violated repeatedly?

Exersice:
- List out the boundaries that you've allowed to be violated.

- For each boundary, note how you feel when it's crossed and how you've responded (or failed to respond).

- Reflect on what changes you need to make to stand firm.

Step 2: Shift from "You" Statements to "I" Statements
Look at Your Communication Patterns
It's time to change how you express your needs. Reflect on conversations where you've felt unheard or misunderstood. Write out a few examples of your "you" statements and rewrite them as "I" statements.

Examples:

- You don't listen to me! → I feel unheard, can we talk?

- You never make time for me! → I miss hanging out with you and would love to spend more time together.

- You don't understand me! → I want you to know me better and hear my perspective.

- You're unhelpful! → I feel stressed and could really use some help right now.

- You don't love me! → I feel uncared for when we don't connect like we used to.

Action Step

- Write down at least 3 "You" statements you commonly use.

- Reword them as "I" statements to express your feelings and needs clearly.

- The next time you're in a similar conversation, use your new "I" statements instead of your usual "You" accusations.

- Notice how the conversation shifts in energy when you take responsibility for your feelings and communicate them directly.

Step 3: Tackling Procrastination

Identify the Fear of Failure

Think about a project or task that you've been procrastinating on—maybe an important work presentation or personal goal. Write down what you fear will happen if you fail.

Example:

- I fear that if I fail, it will prove I'm not good enough.

- I fear that if the presentation goes badly, I'll lose respect from my peers.

Reframe Procrastination

Procrastination isn't just laziness—it's often a defense mechanism. You're trying to protect yourself from failure or rejection. So, let's change how you approach tasks:

Possible Solutions:

- Break the task into smaller, more manageable pieces.

- Start with a 10-minute commitment to reduce the pressure.

- Acknowledge that no matter the outcome, you are valuable. Your worth is not tied to success or failure.

Exersice:

- Choose one task you've been procrastinating on.

- Break it down into small actions. For example, if it's a work presentation, start by outlining the key points or gathering materials.

- Set a timer for 10 minutes, just to start. Once you begin, you'll find the momentum follows.

- Each time you complete a small task, celebrate it. You're taking charge.

Step : 4 Self-Awareness Check-In:

- Did you uncover any areas where your boundaries need improvement?

- How did shifting from "You" to "I" statements affect your interactions?

- What action steps can you take to stop procrastinating and start pursuing your goals, bit by bit?

- How do you feel about standing firm in your boundaries now?

Start with this:

1. **Take Yourself Seriously:** Set at least one non-negotiable boundary today, whether it's about your time, your space, or your emotional energy. No more excuses.

2. **Speak with Certainty**: The next time you communicate a boundary, make sure it's clear, firm, and without hesitation.

3. **Hold People Accountable**: Stop letting people overstep without consequences. If they violate your boundary, be ready to enforce it.

4. **Switch to "I" Statements**: Practice this new communication method daily. Make it a habit to express how you feel instead of accusing others.

5. **Procrastination Busting**: Take that task you've been putting off and break it into 3 small actions. Complete one today.

6. **Embrace Imperfection**: Remind yourself that your value isn't tied to success or failure. You are worthy, always.

> *"Boundaries are not walls. They are the gateways to your peace and purpose. Set them, own them, and watch your life transform."*
> *– Rasesha Rabari*

Let's cut to the chase: **if you lose yourself, you've won nothing**. No amount of success, validation, or applause will ever matter if you can't stand tall in your truth. Life doesn't make sense when you compromise your essence—your unique identity—for the sake of fitting in, pleasing others, or avoiding judgment. This is your life, and you matter.

So, let me ask you: **Who are you**? What is your essence? Are you someone who craves honesty, who wants to speak your mind, who values authenticity? Then own it. But remember, it's not just about speaking—it's about learning how to speak with grace. Sure, you can be blunt or crass, but the moment your delivery clouds your message, your point is lost. True strength is expressing yourself with clarity and confidence while respecting the power of your words.

Here's a truth from my life: **I've made mistakes**. I have faced societal judgments head-on. I've walked through divorce, taken risks. And you know what? I don't regret a thing. These experiences exist, and I've moved past them. You should too. **Don't let the opinions of small-minded people dictate the value of your journey.** Their inability to process life's complexities is a reflection of their limitations, not yours.

You might wonder how I live without guilt. The answer is simple: I don't care about the approval of those who don't matter. My family, friends, and those who genuinely know me—they love me for who I am. Everyone else is just background noise.

Life is yours. You don't owe anyone an explanation for living authentically. The only approval you need is your own. When you embrace this truth, everything changes. You stop apologizing for your mistakes, you stop shrinking to make others comfortable, and you start living boldly.

Here's My Challenge to You:
Take ownership of your life. Right now. Stop compromising your essence for a world that doesn't even understand its own value. Step into your power unapologetically Mistakes? Risks? Judgment? They're not weights to carry—they're badges of honor.

Wear them proudly. Live boldly. And never forget: **"YOU MATTER"**. Now, go own it. **I'm rooting for you.**

— *The One Who Believes in YOU*

"Your essence is your power. Lose it, and
you lose yourself. Embrace it, and you create a
life that's truly yours."
-Rasesha Rabari

Oh, come on—don't tell me you're "too busy" to believe in yourself. Who's the real boss here? Your calendar app or your actual soul?

Putting It All Into Practice

Your Daily Essence Playbook (Exercise)

1. What's your go-to instant happiness fix?

   - Social media

   - Snacking

   - Shopping

   - Other

2. If you had to quit one of these for a week, which would feel impossible?

   - Netflix binge-watching

   - Gaming

   - Junk food cravings

3. If you swapped 30 minutes of social media for a walk, how do you think you'd feel?

   - Energized

   - Bored

   - Relieved

   - Unchanged.

4. What healthy habit do you believe could replace a time-wasting activity?

   - Walking

   - Journaling

   - Reading

   - Meditation

5. Be honest—do you truly think you'd stick to this new habit for a week?

   - Yes! Bring it on.

   - Uhh...maybe.

   - Nope, not happening.

6. What small action gives you a lasting sense of joy?

   - Complimenting someone

   - Taking a deep breath outdoors

   - Writing down your thoughts

   - Dancing to a favorite song.

7. What's been your happiest non-material moment this week?

   - Laughing with a loved one

   - Accomplishing a goal

   - Being in nature

   - Other

8. Did that moment remind you of what truly makes life meaningful?

   - Yes, deeply.

   - A little bit.

   - Honestly, I wasn't paying attention.

9. When was the last time you smiled at something unexpected?

   - Today

   - This week

   - Can't remember

10. Which of these do you most identify with?

   - My career

   - My physical appearance

   - My relationships

   - My possessions

11. If you lost one of the above, how would your sense of self change?

    - Crumble completely

    - Be shaken, but I'd recover

    - I'd be fine—it doesn't define me

12. Are you willing to go a day without mentioning or thinking about something you identify with?

    - Definitely

    - Maybe, but it's hard

    - Not a chance

13. When you stand tall and smile, how does it make you feel?

    - Powerful

    - Silly

    - Unchanged

14. How long could you hold a "power pose" (hands on hips, shoulders back) before feeling ridiculous?

    - Forever—it's empowering!

    - 5 minutes, tops.

    - A few seconds.

15. What's your first go-to when you feel stressed?

- Breathe deeply
- Move your body
- Vent to a friend
- Other

16. Think of a challenging event. Did you view it as:

- A setback
- A lesson
- A blessing in disguise

17. What's the biggest source of clutter in your life?

- Physical junk
- Mental negativity
- Toxic relationships
- All of the above

18. If you could remove one negative element from your life, what would it be?

- A habit
- A person
- An object

19. Who in your life consistently makes you feel valued?

    - A friend

    - A family member

    - A mentor

    - Someone else

20. Have you spent intentional time with these people lately?

    - Yes, regularly

    - Occasionally

    - Not at all

21. Be honest—are there people in your life you'd benefit from seeing less?

    - Absolutely

    - Maybe

    - No

22. How often do you get a full night's rest?

    - Every night

    - A few nights a week

    - Almost never

23. What's your current bedtime routine?

    - Scrolling on my phone
    - Reading or journaling
    - Nothing structured

24. How often do you go to sleep feeling thankful?

    - Every night
    - Occasionally
    - Rarely

25. What emotion are you holding onto the most?

    - Regret
    - Anger
    - Fear
    - Other

26. Are you ready to let that emotion go?

    - Yes, now!
    - Maybe later
    - Not yet

27. When you're stuck in a negative emotion, what helps you snap out of it?

    - Moving
    - Laughing
    - Music
    - Nothing—I stay stuck

28. Did you celebrate a personal victory today?

    - Yes!

    - Not yet, but I will.

    - I never think about that.

29. What kind of story are you writing for yourself right now?

    - A success story

    - A comeback story

    - A stuck-in-neutral story

30. On a scale of 1-10, how much do you truly believe you're important?

    - 1-3: Barely

    - 4-7: I'm getting there

    - 8-10: Fully.

No more excuses. No more waiting for the **"right"** moment. No more doubting whether you're ready. You **"ARE"** ready.

So what are you waiting for? **Come on—get started!** Take that first step, and then the next. Momentum is your superpower.

The life you want is yours for the taking. **Let's go.**

— *I Knows You've Got This*

Your Presence

The Growth

"Your presence is not a reflection of what others think of you; it's a declaration of who you are and the impact you choose to make."
- Rasesha Rabari

In a world often shadowed by negativity, let me remind you the most important & the top priority is you because - **"You Matter"**.

After learning to face the mirror and connect with your essence, you've laid the foundation. You've looked inward, owned your truths, and begun to rebuild. But this is only the start. Now comes the part where you step out of the shadows and into the world—not as a passive participant, but as a force of nature. This is the phase where you realize that your presence in the lives of others isn't optional; it's vital. The way you show up, interact, and inspire is the ripple effect that carries your essence far beyond yourself.

From Mirrors to Windows:

The first tier of life is mastering the mirror — being able to look at yourself without flinching. But it is the second level which will stretch you. It's when you transition from an inward view of yourself to an outward view, which can be seen reflected in the eyes of others. This is where courage meets vulnerability.

It's no longer just about asking, Who am I? Now it's about, Who am I in the lives of those around me?

The truth is, no matter how fiercely independent you might think you are, we are wired for connection. We thrive in relationships, in communities, and in the impact we create in others' lives. But stepping into this world of human connection is not without its challenges.

The Two Types of People:

Let me tell you something hard-hitting: when you step into the world, you will encounter two types of people.

The first type? They're the ones who see others rise and use that as fuel for their own growth. They're inspired, they cheer you on, and they're the wind beneath your wings. These are the people who remind you why connections matter.

Then there's the second type. They see others rise, and instead of taking responsibility for their own growth, they choose to criticize. Why? Because they lack the courage to face their own insecurities. It's easier to tear someone down than to build themselves up. These people will test your boundaries and challenge your strength.

Here's the harsh reality: you can't avoid the second type. You'll meet them at work, in friendships, even in family. But here's the empowering truth: you don't need their approval, and their criticism isn't your truth. What matters is how you choose to respond.

Boundaries Are Bridges

This is where your boundaries come into play. Boundaries are not walls to shut people out; they're bridges to your growth and freedom. They allow you to interact with others without compromising your essence. When you define what you will and won't accept, you protect your energy and align with your purpose.

Respect is non-negotiable. But understand this: not everyone will respect you right away. And that's okay. Because your presence isn't about pleasing everyone—it's about being authentic. It's about living so unapologetically that the right people are drawn to your light and the wrong ones fade into the background.

Why Your Presence Matters:

Your presence is powerful. It's not just about what you say or do—it's about how you make people feel. When you show up as your authentic self, you give others permission to do the same. You become a mirror for their potential.

But here's the kicker: your presence will trigger people. Not everyone is ready to face the mirror you hold up for them. Some will resent you for reminding them of their unfulfilled dreams. Others will celebrate you for inspiring them to rise. Both reactions are gifts. Criticism teaches you resilience; respect teaches you impact.

Sustaining Your Courage:

This tier of living — the "presence" tier — is not simple to maintain. It requires bravery all the time. It's not sufficient to look the mirror in the face once or twice; you have to keep doing it in the eyes of others. And that's where most people mess up.

But here's the truth: courage isn't the absence of fear. It's about experiencing the fear and doing it anyway. It's about picking growth instead of comfort, and integrity instead of acceptance.

Define Your Freedom:

Let me repeat this because it's that important: your boundaries are your freedom. Without them, you risk compromising your essence. And if you lose yourself in the process of pleasing others, you've won nothing.

Boundaries are not selfish; they're necessary. They allow you to preserve your energy, focus on your growth, and protect your peace. And when you operate from a place of peace, you're unstoppable.

- **Before you can show up for others, you must know who you are.** This is the foundation. Without it, your presence will be hollow.

- **Define what you stand for and what you won't tolerate.** Boundaries are not limitations; they're declarations of self-respect.

- **Understand that not everyone will cheer for you, and that's okay.** The ones who matter will rise with you.

- **Showing up as your authentic self takes courage.** It's not a one-time decision; it's a daily commitment.

I believe in you; I see the fire of greatness within you, waiting to be unleashed. You are not here by accident. You are capable of extraordinary things. Step forward boldly, because the world needs your courage, your presence, and your power.

Each day is a crossroads, presenting you with a powerful choice: will you lead your life with intention or let it drift on autopilot? Will you rise to meet your potential or surrender to life's demands? These decisions define who you are and who you will become.

The truth is, life is not easy. The world is full of noise, turbulence, and uncertainty. Everywhere we turn, it feels like there's another storm on the horizon. So many voices try to pull us down, to distract us from our purpose, to drown out the whispers of greatness that reside within us. Yet, it's within this very chaos that we must find our strength.

If you are reading this right now, it's because you too, like me, feel the deep longing to enhance your life, to find meaning, to leave a legacy. You have this undeniable hunger to grow. And it's in this hunger that the power to transform lies.

But how do we navigate this chaotic world? How do we rise above the noise and claim our true potential? The first choice we make each day holds the answer. It is the foundational choice that defines everything else:

Nurturing Relationships

Act of Purpose:

Will we act upon life, or will we simply be acted upon?

Life is a constant flow of events. Some insignificant, others overwhelming. But regardless of what comes our way, we always have a choice: will we let the world push us along like helpless driftwood, or will we seize control, chart our own course, and decide where we are going?

On the surface, the choice seems simple. Of course, we all want to act rather than be passive. Yet, the truth is, many people say they want to take charge of their lives, but when it comes down to it, they hand their power over to external forces—television schedules, the demands of others, the opinions of society. They fall into the trap of letting life happen to them.

But you are different. You are someone who chooses to **act**. You understand that while we cannot control everything that happens to us, we have absolute power over how we respond. You are not a passive bystander in your own life—you are the creator, the architect of your destiny. The key difference between those who thrive and those who merely survive lies in this choice: **to act, not to react**.

Purpose Of Presence:

Acting on life is powerful. But acting without direction? That can lead us astray. Too many people race through life, rushing from task to task, never pausing to ask themselves: What am I doing this for? What is my purpose? It's not enough to be busy. We must be busy with intention.

The second critical choice we make each day is: What purpose will our actions serve? Purpose is the North Star that guides our actions. Without purpose, we drift aimlessly, consumed by the noise, the distractions, and the pressures around us. But when we act with a clear, meaningful purpose—when we align our choices with something larger than ourselves—we step into a new realm of power.

Every action, every decision, must be driven by purpose. Are we striving to build relationships that matter? Are we working towards a career that fulfills us? Are we contributing to the betterment of others and the world around us? The most fulfilled people are those who align their efforts with purpose. They don't waste time chasing empty goals—they pour their energy into pursuits that make a difference.

I challenge you today to examine the purpose behind your actions. Ask yourself: What do I want to stand for? Will your purpose guide you, or will you let the winds of life pull you wherever they may?

Principles Of Presence:

But purpose alone is not enough. Purpose gives us direction, but principles are the map that show us how to get there. Without solid principles, we might start strong, but we will quickly falter when faced with obstacles.

Principles are the non-negotiable truths that guide our lives. They are the bedrock upon which all meaningful action is built. Without them, we lose our way.

In our world, principles like courage, integrity, perseverance, and empathy are the keys to long-term success and fulfillment. These are the principles that fuel our actions and give our lives depth and meaning. The absence of these principles leaves us with a shallow existence, driven by fleeting desires and momentary pleasures.

Let me ask you: **What principles guide your decisions?** Are you living in accordance with your values, or are you swayed by the currents of convenience, popularity, and instant gratification?

Real strength lies in living by these principles, even when it's difficult. True success doesn't come from shortcuts, it comes from a relentless commitment to doing what is right, regardless of the circumstances.

The foundation of a life well-lived is built upon three fundamental choices:

- **Act**:Your willpower in action, your ability to show up and take charge of your life.

- **Purpose**: Your destination, the guiding force behind everything you do.

- **Principles**: Are the means by which you will achieve your goals—your ethical framework, your moral compass.

Each day, you must choose how to show up in the world.

- Will you let life happen to you, or will you take charge of your destiny?

- Will you act with purpose, or will you live on autopilot, reacting to whatever comes your way? And will you commit to principles that elevate your life, or will you succumb to the pressures of the world?

The Dance of Patience and Love:
A Story of Presence

On a quiet morning, beneath the golden glow of the rising sun, Patience and Love made a pact. They agreed to meet at a specific time and place: beneath the 23rd tree in an expansive, lush farm. The air was crisp, carrying the earthy aroma of soil and dew. It was a setting of peace, a stage prepared for something profound.

Patience arrived promptly, her heart steady and her spirit grounded. She glanced up at the towering 23rd tree—a monument of time and growth—and allowed herself to settle into its shade. The wind whispered through the leaves, as if urging her to wait with calm assurance.

But as the minutes ticked by, Patience grew uneasy. She checked her watch. Then the horizon. Then the watch again. The stillness around her felt heavy, and doubt began to creep into her mind. **Was it the 23rd tree? Or could it have been the 56th?**

The thought took root, and with it came urgency. **What if I'm in the wrong place?** she thought. Determined to take control, she rose and walked briskly toward the 56th tree. It wasn't far, but the journey felt like forever—because now, doubt had replaced her calm.

When Love Arrives

Meanwhile, Love appeared. He approached the 23rd tree, the very place they had agreed upon. His presence radiated warmth, a quiet power that seemed to make everything around him come alive. But as he looked around, Patience was nowhere to be seen.

He waited. He leaned against the tree, listening to the rustle of leaves and the distant calls of birds. The moments stretched, and though he stayed still, his mind began to wander.

Was this the wrong tree? he wondered. Maybe he had misunderstood. Perhaps she had said the 56th tree instead of the 23rd. Love, for all his strength and longing, began to second-guess himself. He stood for a moment longer, then decided to move. **Maybe she's waiting for me somewhere else**, he thought as he drifted away.

The Almosts

Patience reached the 56th tree, her eyes scanning every shadow, every branch. But Love was not there. Frustration began to build. **Why isn't he here? Why isn't this simple?** she thought.

And yet, neither was willing to give up entirely. Both began wandering aimlessly around the farm, each searching for the other. Their paths crossed so closely that they could have brushed shoulders, but they never truly met.

It was as if fate had laid a thread between them, pulling them near but never allowing it to tie the knot. They were caught in a dance of almost—always close, but never close enough.

The Return to the Beginning

Finally, after hours of searching and spiraling through confusion, Patience found herself back beneath the 23rd tree. Exhausted, she sank to the ground. What was the point? she thought. Maybe Love isn't meant for me. Maybe I've been chasing something that doesn't exist.

Her heart ached with the weight of disappointment. But as she sat there, something remarkable happened. She let go. She released the need to control, to chase, to figure it all out. At that moment, she simply existed. Barely a minute passed when she felt a gentle tap on her shoulder. She turned, and there he was—Love.

"Where have you been?" she asked, her voice trembling. "I've been searching for you everywhere."

Love smiled softly. **"Stop looking for me, and I will find you,"** he said.

The Lesson in Their Meeting

Patience and Love finally stood together, beneath the very tree they had first agreed upon. But their journey was not without lessons. Their wandering, their missteps, their near-misses—these were not failures.

They were reflections of the truths we all face when navigating life and relationships.

Here's the heart of it: **Patience lacked sensitivity in her quest for Love.** She was quick to abandon the place of trust, scared of the stillness it demanded. Her fear of waiting, of committing fully to the process, led her to second-guess and move too soon. And Love? Love hesitated when confronted with uncertainty. Though powerful and steady, he allowed doubt to pull him away from where he was meant to be. Together, they reveal a dance we all know too well: the delicate balance of trust and action, of staying and moving, of faith and fear.

The Missing Sensitivity in Love

1. **The Rush to Close the Door**: In relationships, many of us are like Patience—quick to close the door at the first sign of discomfort or delay. We forget that love, like life, requires staying power. The capacity to endure uncertainty is a mark of emotional strength.

2. **The Fear of Commitment**: Love, too, can falter. It can be hesitant, scared of rooting itself too deeply. But without commitment—without choosing to stay rooted—love drifts, untethered and unfulfilled.

3. **The Myth of Perfection**: Both Patience and Love struggled because they were searching for perfection. But here's the truth: there is no perfect person, no perfect moment, no perfect place. The beauty of love is in its imperfection—in the messy, raw, and real process of growth.

4. **The Lack of Faith**: Patience forgot to hold faith. In her rush to find answers, she lost sight of the fact that some things take time to unfold. Love, too, failed to trust that staying still was the right choice.

What This Means for You

This story is more than just a tale about two abstract forces. It's a mirror. It reflects the struggles we face in our relationships—with others and with ourselves.

How often do you, like Patience, abandon a relationship, a dream, or a commitment because waiting feels unbearable? How often do you, like Love, hesitate to stay because doubt whispers that you might be in the wrong place?

The truth is, meaningful relationships—be they romantic, familial, or platonic—require both patience and love. They require the willingness to wait and the courage to stay. They demand that we let go of the perfection box and embrace the messy, beautiful reality of human connection.

Patience and Love ultimately met because Patience stopped chasing, and Love stopped wandering. They returned to the place where they had started. And isn't that the greatest irony of all? That often, what we're searching for is right where we began—but it takes the journey to see it.

In your relationships, don't rush to close the door when things get hard. Don't run from stillness. And don't let doubt convince you to abandon the place where you're meant to be.

Hold faith. Stay rooted. Let love find you—not because you're perfect, but because you're present.

And remember, **the privilege of your presence is not in what you do, but in how you do**. The world needs you—not your perfection, but your authenticity, your grace, and your heart.

Now go out there and claim the stage where you've earned it. Stop searching and start being. **Love will find you when you stop chasing and start trusting.**

> *"Love isn't about finding someone who completes you; it's about finding someone who inspires you to be complete on your own." -Rasesha Rabari*

This story my English teacher, Mrs. Shaikh, once shared that changed how I see love and life. It was about Patience and Love—a story of presence, timing, and trust. It taught me something profound: **we rush for love as if it's now or never, forgetting that love isn't a destination—it's a reflection of who we are.**

We chase love, convinced that its absence diminishes us, and when it doesn't show up the way we hope, we drown in self-doubt. Rejection feels like a blow to our worth, but here's the truth: **your value isn't tied to anyone's ability to love you.** Love is your ability, your light, your reflection. And not everyone possesses the capacity to meet it—and that's okay.

Don't let rejection bury your self-worth. Let it remind you of the power within you—the power to love, to trust, and to wait. Because the right love doesn't require you to chase or compromise who you are. It will find you, just as you are, when the time is right.

So pause. Breathe. Trust. Love is within you—and when you honor that, it will always find its way back to you.

With belief in your journey.
When you stand firm in who you are, you send a clear message to the world: "I will no longer settle." And that's not just about love—it's about every interaction and decision in your life. The moment you stop entertaining what drains you, the right people, opportunities, and experiences will begin to flow into your life.

But let's get something straight: the wrong ones aren't always "bad." Sometimes, they're just not right for you. And that's okay. Their capacity to see your worth might be limited, not because they're malicious, but because they don't see the fullness of themselves. When you show up for others more than they show up for you, you create a cycle where your efforts are taken for granted. You paint their reds into greens, hoping they'll change—but the truth is, **change has to come from within them**. Your role is not to rescue; your role is to stand tall in your truth.

The Fear That Holds You Back

Who's to blame for your heartbreak or disappointment? It's not your emotions, and it's not always the people around you. More often than not, it's your fear—fear of aiming higher, fear of stepping out of your comfort zone, and fear of demanding what you truly deserve.

It's your fear that convinces you to settle. It whispers lies like, "What if no one else comes along? What if you're not enough?" But let me tell you something: fear is a terrible advisor. When you let fear dictate your choices, you shrink into a version of yourself that's less than what you're meant to be.

The right one will come—not when you're chasing, convincing, or settling—but when you've made room for them. And that room can only be created by clearing out what doesn't serve you.

The Power of Being Alone

Here's a hard truth: if you can't find peace within yourself, you'll never find it in another person. Real love starts with self-love. And self-love isn't just about bubble baths and affirmations; it's about being at peace in your own company. It's about knowing that your happiness isn't dependent on anyone else because it comes from within.

The capacity to be alone is the capacity to love. Why? Because when you're comfortable being by yourself, you're no longer looking to fill a void. You're not clinging to someone out of fear or insecurity. Instead, you're choosing to be with someone because they complement your life—not complete it.

Think about it: what are you trading your energy for? Are you giving it to people who make you question your worth? Are you investing it in relationships that are built on uncertainty and fear? Stop settling for situationships or half-hearted commitments. You deserve someone who sees you, respects you, and matches your energy.

What Real Love Looks Like

Let's talk about love—real love. Not the Hollywood version, not the fairy tale, but the raw, unfiltered truth. Real love isn't blind. Infatuation is blind. Lust is blind. But love? Love sees. Love sees every flaw, every fear, and every insecurity—and it stays. It doesn't mean love is easy, but it's real.

Love doesn't make you feel small or insecure. It doesn't leave you questioning your worth. If it does, then it's not love—it's a lesson. Real love builds you up. It's about two people who see each other fully and choose to grow together.

But here's the thing: nobody is going to love you exactly the way you want to be loved. That's not a bad thing—it's reality. People love based on their capacity, and that capacity is shaped by their upbringing, experiences, and self-awareness. If someone hasn't done the work to know themselves, how can they possibly meet you where you are?

Infatuation V/S Love

They say love is blind. I say, "No way." Infatuation is blind—blind to flaws, blind to challenges, blind to reality. Love is the opposite. Love is seeing everything—the good, the bad, the ugly—and choosing to embrace it anyway.

- **Infatuation** breaks at the first sign of imperfection.
- **Love** grows stronger through challenges.
- **Infatuation** is fragile, demanding, and conditional.
- **Love** is resilient, giving, and unconditional.

True love isn't about perfection. It's about seeing someone's imperfections and saying, "I choose you anyway."

The Courage to Show Up Fully

Love is a courageous act. It requires vulnerability, accountability, and strength. Cowards can't commit to real love because it demands too much—it demands integrity, loyalty, effort, and the willingness to show up fully.

So, where do you stand? Are you settling for something less because it's comfortable? Or are you stepping into your presence and demanding the love you know you deserve? Remember this: "**They are not what they say; they are what you do.** "Their actions define what your presence means to them. The way they handle relationships, says a lot about their mentality. It's time you stand up for yourself and speak volumes. If you're constantly compromising your standards, you're telling the world—and yourself—that you don't believe in your own worth. And that has to stop today.

At the end of the day, love is about more than just a relationship.

You matter - Your relationship matters: When you know your worth, the world will have no choice but to reflect it back to you.

Life isn't just about the people you date or the romantic relationships you pursue. It's about everyone you choose to let into your world. The ones you grant access to your thoughts, your energy, and your heart.

This brings us to an important truth: **who you allow into your life determines the quality of your experiences**. Don't waste your energy trying to make the wrong people right for you. It's not your job to fix them. Let them walk their path while you focus on yours.

You are not alone: Many of us carry wounds from unreasonable experiences. But these moments don't define you—they refine you.

Let me share something personal that might hit close to home. I've fed mouths that whispered behind my back. I've wiped tears from faces that caused my own to fall. I've picked up people who worked to knock me down. I've done favors for those who could never return them. And I've stood by people who wouldn't stand by me. Sound familiar?

I don't regret it. Why? Because bitterness has no place in my soul. I won't let the actions of others dim my light or twist my character. Staying authentic— staying kind—isn't always easy in a world that can feel harsh and unforgiving. But the truth is, being true to yourself takes far more strength than retreating into resentment.

Your power isn't in the walls you build to protect yourself. It's in your ability to rise above what tries to break you. You're stronger than you think, and the world needs the light only you can bring. So hold onto it, fiercely and unapologetically, because even when others take you for granted, your kindness is your legacy.

Remember this: Your courage to keep shining will always outlast their shadows.

Acting with Purpose and Possibility

Are You Motivated by Necessity or Possibility?

Motivation is the driving force that pushes us forward. But what drives you? Are you pushed by necessity, by the need to survive, or are you pulled by the possibility of what could be? It's an important question, one that can reshape the course of your life.

There are two kinds of people in the world: those who are motivated by necessity, and those who are motivated by possibility

- People motivated by necessity are driven by what they have to do. They live in response to life's demands. They go to work because they must. They buy what they need. They make decisions based on what's available, rather than what's possible.

It's not bad to be motivated by necessity—after all, necessity has its place. But it's a limited form of motivation. It often keeps you stuck in a cycle of reacting, instead of creating.

- Then, there are those who are motivated by possibility. They look at the world and see endless opportunities. They ask not what they have to do, but what theywant to do. They don't settle for what's available—they strive for what's possible. They move toward potential, they embrace uncertainty, and they constantly seek to expand the boundaries of their experience.

The truth is, there's no one-size-fits-all approach to motivation. Both necessity and possibility have their places. Some jobs require you to focus on the now, to attend to detail, and to maintain stability. But when you're looking to grow, to innovate, or to push boundaries, it's the pull of possibility that will light your path.

Think about the difference between a worker who simply shows up because it's necessary and one who shows up because they see potential. The first person may be reliable, but the second person will be the catalyst for change. They will be the one who challenges the status quo and creates something new.

Are you driven by necessity or possibility? The answer will determine the kind of life you lead. The choice is yours. You can choose to live for what's required, or you can choose to live for what's possible. And in doing so, you choose the path to greatness.

Applying Power of Possibility

Understanding the difference between necessity and possibility isn't just about you—it's also about the people you lead. This principle works in every area of life. If you're an employer, a teacher, or a parent, you need to understand the motivations that drive those around you.

The point is, everyone is different. Some people are motivated by what they must do, and some are motivated by what they can do. Understanding this distinction helps you to create a more meaningful and effective path, whether you're motivating yourself or others.

Know What Drives You

Ultimately, the most powerful thing you can do is understand your own motivations. Are you living your life based on necessity, or are you following the pull of possibility? Are you creating your future, or are you reacting to what life hands you?

The key is to embrace possibility, but to also know when necessity must come into play. Life is not all about chasing dreams; sometimes it's about showing up and doing the work that needs to be done. But if you want to live a life of fulfillment, a life of impact, a life where you leave a legacy—you must allow yourself to be driven by the possibilities that lie ahead.

And if you're willing to step into your power, if you're willing to be led by the pull of possibility, there is no limit to what you can achieve.

You matter. Your presence matters. Your choices matter; Every single day, you are shaping the world around you, and the world needs you to show up fully, with all of your heart, your energy, and your brilliance. The challenge is to wake up every day and choose to be driven by the pull of possibility. Choose to be the person who sees the future not as something that happens to you, but as something you create.

I hope this message ignites something deep inside of you. I hope it encourages you to act with courage, with intention, and with the unwavering belief that you are worthy of everything you desire in this life.

Embrace the possibility of who you are becoming, and know that you are not alone on this journey. Together, we can create a future defined not by necessity, but by the infinite possibilities before us.

> *"When you embrace the pull of possibility, the world shifts beneath your feet—no longer a place of limitation, but a vast expanse of opportunity waiting for you to step into your power." - Rasesha Rabari*

The Deep Understanding:

Every person you meet is carrying something—a dream they haven't dared to share, an insecurity they're afraid will be exposed, or a battle they're fighting in silence. Most of us rush through life so preoccupied with our own concerns that we miss the opportunity to connect at a deeper level.

But when you stop and choose to see beyond the surface, something changes. People don't just hear you; they feel you. They sense your authenticity, your care, and your presence. Suddenly, you're no longer just a participant in their story—you become a meaningful chapter in their journey.

- **People are often insecure**. How many people do you meet who are silently doubting themselves, questioning their worth, or feeling unsure of their place in the world? Offer them confidence. Be the one who sees their strengths and isn't afraid to say so. Give them the gift of believing in them, especially when they struggle to believe in themselves.

- **People want to feel special**. Compliments are cheap when they're fake or shallow. But a sincere acknowledgment? That's gold. Look for something real, something meaningful, and compliment them on it. Make them feel valued, seen, and special—

not because it benefits you but because everyone deserves to feel valued.

- **People desire a better tomorrow.** It's human nature to hope for more. A brighter future, a bigger dream. When you show others that there's hope, that you believe in their future, you become a beacon for them. You show them that no matter how challenging the present, there's something beautiful to look forward to.

- **People need to be understood**. The simplest way to make someone feel understood? Listen. Not just with your ears, but with your heart. Listen without judging, without interrupting, without letting your mind drift to what you'll say next. Be the person who listens deeply, and you'll build bonds that withstand time.

- **People can be selfish**. This isn't a criticism—it's human nature. We're wired to think about our own needs first. So, speak to those needs. Show people how you're aligned with what they care about. Approach them with empathy, meeting them where they are rather than where you want them to be.

- **People get emotionally low**. Life has a way of knocking people down. When they're in a dark place, you can be the light. Encourage them, uplift them. Be the person who doesn't just say, "I'm here," but truly shows up when they're struggling.

- **People want to be associated with success**. Help them win, not just for yourself, but for them. When you help others succeed, their victories become part of your legacy too. Let your support be the difference between them giving up and pressing forward.

Loving People for Who They Are

People are messy—complicated, flawed, sometimes selfish. But here's the truth: you're not here to fix or judge them; you're here to connect.

- **Understanding isn't agreeing**. You don't have to sign off on every decision someone makes.

- **Understanding isn't fixing**. You're not their superhero. Save the cape for your own growth.

- **Understanding is connection**. It's about saying, "I see you, as you are, and you matter to me."

But let's flip the mirror for a second: are you taking yourself into account? If you're ignoring your own emotions, flaws, and tendencies, you're just projecting your insecurities onto the world. You're not engaging—you're reacting.

Here's the hard truth: we judge ourselves by our intentions but judge others by their actions. That's not fair, but it's human. To transform your relationships, start with you. Know your desires, strengths, and flaws. When you understand yourself, you'll finally have the foundation to respect others and influence your life in powerful, lasting ways.

The Value of Relationships

"If you have to ask for it, it loses its value." Think about that. True relationships—friendship, love, partnership—aren't transactions. You don't keep a scorecard or negotiate emotional IOUs.

Relationships are investments. You put in trust, emotions, and effort, and you build confidence in the bond that the other person chooses to stay.

Now listen carefully: if someone loses you because of their own stupidity, that's their loss, not your burden. Don't be nice and cling to dead weight. Be smart enough to let them go. Stop craving the people who clearly don't value you.

Here's the rule: Letting go isn't cruelty—it's clarity. The ones who see your worth won't make you ask for it. Keep your standards high, and your circle full of people who choose to be there for you.

Balancing Presence and Influence

The Four Powers Within You:

We are all each bestowed with these 4 incredible gifts:

Self-awareness – The capacity to examine your own ideas, feelings, and actions.

Imagination — The ability to visualize possibilities beyond your current reality.

Conscience – Your internal voice that leads you to the choice you know is right.

Willpower – The ability to do what matters in the presence of resistance.

These gifts, when balanced, can create incredible harmony. But if one is missing, imbalance occurs. Consider history's warning: Adolf Hitler possessed immense self-awareness, imagination, and willpower.

Yet, he lacked conscience, and the results were catastrophic. His example reminds us that your brain can be driven by influence, but your heart must be guided by conscience.

The Sphere of Action vs. The Sphere of Worry

Life is full of things we care about but can't control. Let's call these your Sphere of Worry.It includes external events, others' opinions, or things that seem unfair. When you pour your energy here, you feel drained, stuck, and frustrated. Why? Because no amount of effort will change what's outside your control.

Now, focus on the Sphere of Action. This is where your power lies: your thoughts, your responses, your choices. When you pour energy here, you reclaim control. You start influencing outcomes, building momentum, and expanding your ability to impact your world.

Here's the magic: as you expand your Sphere of Action, your Sphere of Worry shrinks. Why? Because action builds confidence, confidence fuels progress, and progress redefines what's possible.

Ask yourself:

Am I spending my energy where it matters most?

What small action can I take today to shift my focus to what I can control?

Redefine Responsibility: Response-Ability
Responsibility doesn't imply blame or a burden. It's about freedom. Break this down: response-ability — the ability to respond, to choose your response in any situation. Nobody can take that from you.

You lose your power when you react in the moment. But when you step back, take stock then move with purpose, you take back your power.

Remember, your response sets an example for others. By staying focused, you inspire your family, friends, and community to do the same. Your courage becomes contagious.

Build Trust with Every Choice
Relationships thrive on trust, and trust is like a vault. Every time you act with integrity, kindness, or loyalty, you make investments. Every time you lie, criticize, or betray, you make withdrawals. A full vault means strong relationships that can weather conflict. An overdrawn vault means constant tension, miscommunication, and mistrust.

Here's how to fill the vault:
- Show up when it matters most.
- Listen to understand, not just to reply.
- Apologize sincerely and forgive quickly.
- Defend those who aren't in the room.

Trust isn't built overnight, but every small choice you make contributes to the balance. Build your emotional life on your own strength, and you'll remain unshaken regardless of how others treat you.

Opportunity to Invest:
Every challenge in life is an opportunity to grow closer to those around you:

- When someone is having a bad day, offer kindness instead of criticism.

- When someone makes a mistake, offer forgiveness instead of resentment.

- When you hear gossip, stay loyal to the absent.

Each action strengthens your vault of trust. You're not just reacting to life; you're transforming it, one choice at a time.

Nourishment:
Science shows that humans need forms of nourishment daily—what we'll call "hugs." These don't have to be physical; they can be verbal affirmations, acts of service, or moments of quiet connection. Hugs can even come from prayer, meditation, or self-care.

Giving or receiving hugs include:

- A heartfelt compliment.

- An undistracted conversation.

- Writing a thank-you note to someone you appreciate.

- Offering a moment of stillness and gratitude to yourself.

Watch how your energy shifts and your relationships deepen.

- **Sphere of Worry** → Sphere of Action: Shift focus to what you can control.

- **Trust Vault:** Invest in your relationships with consistent loyalty, honesty, and love.

- **Response-Ability**: Reclaim your power by choosing your response in any situation.

- **Nourishment**: Feed your emotional and spiritual needs daily.

Ask yourself:
- Which sphere do you spend most of your energy on—Action or Worry?

- What is one action you can take today to make a trust deposit in a key relationship?

- How can you give or receive hugs today onwards?

"Your power isn't in controlling others—it's in mastering yourself. Focus inward, act boldly, and let your example lead the way." -Rasesha Rabari

You matter because your choices matter. You have the power to influence not only your own life but the lives of everyone you touch. **Focus on your gifts. Expand your Sphere of Action. Nourish your relationships. And always remember: You are responsible, capable, and unstoppable.**

The Fine Line: Involving vs. Interfering

As you deepen your presence in someone's life, there's a delicate balance to strike—a thin line between **involvement** and **interference**.

To interfere is to overstep. It's when we impose our opinions, insert ourselves into situations we don't belong to, or try to fix problems that aren't ours to solve. Even when done with good intentions, interference can feel suffocating. It robs people of their autonomy, their grace, and their ability to navigate their own story.

To involve is to support. It's choosing to be present without taking over. It's holding space for someone while trusting them to lead their own journey. Involvement is an act of humility—it acknowledges that while you're there to help, you're not the hero of their story.

Sometimes, the most powerful thing you can do for someone isn't offering advice or solutions. It's simply being there. A steady hand. A calm voice. A nonjudgmental presence.

Don't Overplay Your Role

Here's the truth: **you can't save people from their battles**. Those battles are theirs to fight, and their growth depends on it. Your role isn't to shield them from struggle—it's to walk beside them, offering support without overshadowing their strength.

Think of yourself as the best man at a wedding. Your job isn't to take center stage; it's to stand in the wings, ready to assist, encourage, and celebrate. It's their moment, not yours.

When you overplay your role, you risk becoming a source of pressure rather than peace. But when you choose involvement over interference, you create space for trust, respect, and mutual growth.

Want to leave a lasting impact on someone's life? Master the art of presence.

Here's how:

- **Offer Unconditional Support**. Be the person who shows up—not just when it's easy, but when it's uncomfortable. Your consistency will speak volumes.

- **Choose Empathy Over Judgment.** Before you respond, ask yourself: Am I here to help or to criticize? Empathy builds bridges, while judgment erects walls.

- **Respect Their Journey**. Everyone's path is different. Even if you don't understand their choices, honor their right to make them.

- **Know When to Step Back**. There's a time to offer help and a time to let go. Trust in their ability to rise, even when it's hard to watch.

You Cannot Do It Alone;

Let's shatter a lie that has been fed to us for far too long: the myth of independence. The world loves to celebrate the idea of the "self-made" person, the lone warrior who achieved greatness on their own. But here's the brutal truth: nobody achieves greatness alone. Nobody heals alone. Nobody thrives alone.

True strength is not about standing alone—it's about standing together. It's about knowing when to lean on your tribe and when to become the pillar for someone else. The strength of community, the power of human connection, is what drives us forward. We are wired for connection, and the most powerful thing you can do is embrace that truth.

But here's the hard reality: not everyone deserves a seat at your table.

The people you allow into your life have the power to either elevate you or drain you. Your inner circle should be a fortress, built with intention, love, and respect. You hold the power to choose who gets in.

Surround yourself with those who love you for who you are, not for what you have. In a world where masks are worn to fit in, choosing the right people can be a real struggle—but it's a struggle worth fighting for.

Yes, you'll make mistakes. Yes, you'll trust the wrong people. But the key is knowing when to get off the wrong train. The longer you stay, the more energy you waste trying to fix something that was never meant to be. Broken trust hurts, but it also teaches you valuable lessons. It teaches you to honor yourself, to trust your intuition, to set boundaries, and to enforce them with courage.

And here's a powerful reminder from one of my favorite songs:

"If I could love the wrong one this much... just imagine when the right one shows up."

Section 4

Forgiveness and Inner Strength

The Struggle for Intrinsic Worth

Many people go through life yearning for validation because they've never experienced unconditional love or developed an intrinsic sense of self-worth. They seek approval and recognition to fill a deep, hollow void. This emptiness often drives them to borrow strength from external sources like power, wealth, status, or reputation. But here's the truth: none of these will ever be enough.

The need for external validation is a distraction from doing the real work—learning to love yourself, flaws and all. Forgiveness, both of others and of yourself, is the gateway to this kind of love. It allows you to let go of the false narratives that say you aren't enough or that your worth depends on others' approval. Instead, it anchors you in the truth that your value is inherent and infinite.

Courage in Forgiveness

Forgiveness isn't about letting them off the hook—it's about freeing yourself. Imagine taking the knife out of your back, not to stab someone else, but to heal. That's what forgiveness is: **freedom**.

Let's be crystal clear:

- Forgiveness isn't weakness. **It's courage**.

- Forgiveness doesn't excuse injustice. It declares, **"You don't get to control my peace."**

Forgiveness is reclaiming your power, saying, **"I choose me over the pain."**

Let go, not because they deserve it, but because you do. Choose forgiveness without sacrificing your boundaries. **You can forgive someone and still deny them access to your life**. Letting go doesn't mean clinging to hope for their change—it means choosing your own growth.

The Fine Line: Letting Go and Forgiving

Forgiveness is a two-way street. If someone truly wants it, they'll take accountability. They'll own their mess, apologize deeply, and mean it. But even if they don't? You can still choose forgiveness—for you.

Don't mistake forgiveness for being a doormat. **You don't owe anyone your peace.** You can love someone and still let them go. That's not cold; that's clarity.

The Brutal Truth About Waiting

Stop waiting for people who aren't coming back. **"I miss you" doesn't mean "I'm returning." "I love you" doesn't mean "I'll stay."** Holding out for someone to realize they can't live without you is wasting the life you should be living.

Life isn't a movie. There's no skipping the painful chapters. You've got to live every page, meet every character, and yes, endure the heart-wrenching moments. But that's the beauty of your story—it's yours.

Let the pain write its chapter, but don't let it define your book.

"Your story isn't about who hurt you—it's about how you rose above." - Rasesha Rabari

Being the Change You Want to See

To create deep connections you need to first be the person you want to attract.

If you desire grace, be gracious first. If you want honesty, be honest — even when it's uncomfortable. Begin with practicing self-respect if you want respect. You, your actions, your choices, your words have to mirror the kind of person with whom you want to be surrounded by.

Your presence ought to reflect your values. It's about being present — each and every time, with integrity, courage and love. You have to be the change you wish to see in others. Lead by example. Be the first to extend grace, the first to forgive, the first to love.

Here's the secret: People might forget what you said, and they might forget what you did — but they will never forget how you made them feel.

And you have the ability to make others feel seen, heard and valued. Build a safe space for people to be themselves. Share non-judgmental space. Be present. By doing this, you aren't merely building relationships but rather a legacy, a legacy of connection, compassion, and love.

Give Without Expectations

In a transactional world, giving without expecting anything in return is an act of rebellion. When you show up for others without an agenda, it opens the door to authentic, meaningful relationships. This isn't about recognition or reciprocation — it's about living in alignment with your values. Give, because that's who you are. You give because in giving, you set off a chain reaction of love, kindness, and connection that will return to you in ways you cannot imagine.

The act of giving opens up possibilities and creates bonds that transcend ordinary exchanges. It's a powerful force, one that strengthens your community and brings you closer to your highest purpose.

This is the real definition of greatness. It is possible for us to leave a legacy of riches, fame, and accomplishments. But these have a way of fading over time. It's not what you do that matters, but how you make others feel — how you impact their hearts and lives.

Don't chase fame or recognition. They are not going to linger into eternity. Instead, try to leave a mark on people's hearts.

Carve your name not in stone, make an impression in the hearts of all who meet you. Be the person who picks other people up, who sees them, hears them, values them. What you have and where you have been will not determine your legacy but who you have become as a person and how you have made others feel.

This is the greatness that lasts. This is the kind of legacy that lasts.

And as you go on with your life, always remember this: The people that are behind the crowd are not the ones that make the biggest impact. It's the ones who walk beside others, the ones who give without condition, who love without reservation, who decide to show up for each other, day after day.

Every relationship you build, every life you touch is a part of your lasting legacy. This story and what you do with it matters, you matter – the world needs you to show up, to be real, to connect, and to create a future of love and human connection that we can dream of.

It starts with you to be the change you want to see.

Hey No Matter What—you're not just living your life in isolation.

You're a force in the lives of everyone around you. But hey, no pressure, right? (Kidding, ALL the pressure.)

Section 5

Putting It All Into Practice

Your Daily Presence Playbook

1. STOP Over-Apologizing

"Sorry for existing!" ...Seriously? Just say, "Thank you for understanding" and move on.

2. Check Your Energy Leaks

If someone's draining you like a cheap battery, it's time to unplug.

3. Learn the Art of the Big, Fat 'No'

Don't tell me you're saying yes to stuff you hate. No is a complete sentence. Use it.

4. Compliment Someone—Without Expecting a Return Favor

Giving feels good. Do it because YOU want to, not because you're fishing for one back.

5. Drop the "Should" Mentality

"I should call them even though they make me miserable..." STOP. Do what feels authentic, not obligatory.

6. Take the Mirror Test

Before helping someone, ask yourself: Am I showing up for ME first? If not, pause.

7. Laugh at Yourself—Loudly

Tripped over nothing? Forgot your keys? Who cares? Embrace your humanity.

8. Let Go of the "Fix-It" Mentality

You're not here to solve everyone's problems. Be a support, not a superhero.

9. Set Social Media Boundaries

Seriously, if scrolling leaves you feeling like a potato, cut it off.

10. Be Present, Not Perfect

Nobody's impressed by your "always-busy" badge. Show up, fully, even if it's messy.

11. Celebrate Someone Else's Win

Jealousy? Don't tell me you're letting that petty voice win. Celebrate them—it lifts you both.

12. Stop Explaining Your Choices

"I'm doing this because…" NOPE. Your life, your call. End of story.

13. Turn Off the News (for Real)

If it's wrecking your vibe, unplug. The world won't implode if you skip a headline.

14. Practice the 3-Second Rule

Feel an emotional gut punch? Pause. Breathe. Respond. Don't let reactive you take the wheel.

15. Forgive, but Don't Forget Yourself in the Process

Forgiving doesn't mean inviting toxic people back into your life. Let go, but set boundaries.

16. Redefine Success

Who said it's a big house or a million followers? Define what it looks like for YOU.

17. Rest Is Not Weakness

If you're running on fumes, STOP. Rest isn't optional; it's survival.

18. Ditch the Drama

Love stirring the pot? Don't tell me you enjoy the aftertaste. Drama's overrated.

19. Ask for Help Without the Guilt Trip

Need a hand? Say it. Strong people ask; martyrs don't.

20. Own Your Flaws

That quirk you hate? Someone else thinks it's amazing. Embrace it.

21. Don't Take Their Mood Personally

If someone's grumpy, it's not your fault. Stop carrying their baggage.

22. Grieve Without the Deadline

Loss takes time. Feel it fully—there's no expiration date on healing.

23. Give Space to Grow

You're evolving, so is everyone else. Allow it, even if it's uncomfortable.

24. Cut the Comparison Crap

Scrolling your ex-classmate's "perfect" life? STOP. Your journey is YOURS. Period.

25. Invest in Quality Over Quantity

Friends? Clothes? Energy? Choose depth over numbers. Every time.

26. Speak Your Truth—Loudly

Quiet isn't the same as peace. Say what needs saying, unapologetically.

27. Thank Your Past Self

The mistakes, the wins, the cringe moments—they shaped you. Celebrate them all.

28. Notice Your "Why"

Are you doing it for love or validation? Check your motives and adjust accordingly.

29. Forgive Yourself Daily

Forgot something? Messed up? Join the club. Self-forgiveness is power.

30. Remember This: Your Presence Changes Lives

Don't tell me you're doubting this. You showing up—authentically—is the gift the world needs. Believe it.

The role you play in others' lives is a reflection of how you treat yourself.

So, stop overthinking. Start owning. Your presence matters. "YOU MATTER". And the world is a better place because of it.

Now, go show them what you're made of. You've got this.

Your Power

The Bloom

Your Essence × Your Presence = Your Power

Power is not given to you by the world. This is not a present, tied with a bow of applause or approval from someone else. Real power is inner — something that you create. It's born from your essence, the unshakeable core of you that can never be altered, and your presence, the energy and intention you emit into the world. When these two forces come together, they multiply exponentially.

Your essence is the authentic self that cannot be shaken. It's your values, your beliefs, your truth — who you are when no one's watching. It is the aspect of you that never changes, even as life attempts to engage you in a thousand different directions. You are drawn to truth in a world of lies, honesty in a world of deception, Your essence is clarity in confusion, strength in vulnerability, and light in the darkest times.

Your presence is how you bring that essence to life. This is not simply about visibility; it's about presence. It's a conscious decision to let your inner truth radiate out, with conviction and grace.

Your aura is how you own a room without saying a single word. It's how you carry yourself, the energy that you give off, the way your doings are aligned with your principles.

That intersection of your essence and your presence becomes a magnetic force for whatever is to come in your life. This is your power. It's not loud —it's magnetic. It commands respect, trust, and influence because it is grounded in authenticity.

Your Power is Your Responsibility

There's a certain magic in embracing your power. Not the kind that craves dominance or seeks to overpower, but the kind that rises after every fall, fueled by values that anchor you in truth and purpose. Your power is the strength to choose grace over revenge, clarity over confusion. It's the quiet confidence of knowing your worth so deeply that no one can diminish it.

But here's the thing: power demands responsibility. It's not about suppressing yourself for the comfort of others. It's about standing in your light unapologetically and creating a lasting impact through the imprint of your presence. Zero tolerance for disrespect is not arrogance; it's alignment with self-respect. Spirituality and humility are not excuses to abandon your boundaries. They're tools to reinforce them. When you own your power, you inspire others to do the same.

The Story of the Snake and the Priest

Once, in a humble village surrounded by dense forests, a traveling priest became known for his wisdom and teachings on spirituality. He wandered from village to village, sharing profound insights on love, kindness, and the importance of values. His words had the power to shift mindsets and awaken dormant courage.

Years later, the priest returned to a village where his teachings had once resonated deeply. As he walked through a dusty trail, he noticed a snake lying in the shade of a tree. It was a pitiful sight—the snake that had once been feared and admired for its glimmering scales and formidable size was now thin, bruised, and lifeless in its demeanor.

The priest approached, his heart heavy with concern. "What happened to you?" he asked. "The last time I was here, you were magnificent—strong, shiny, and respected by all."

The snake lifted its head weakly and sighed. "I heard your words that day. You were preaching to the villagers, telling them to live with kindness and refrain from causing harm. I was hiding in the bushes, listening. You didn't know I was there, but your words struck a chord within me. I decided I would no longer bite anyone. I wanted to embody the values you spoke of."

The priest listened intently as the snake continued. "Since then, I've let go of my old ways. Even when children threw stones at me or villagers mocked me, I didn't retaliate. I kept my promise to myself. But look at me now. They trample over me without fear. They hurt me without consequence. I've been reduced to this miserable state."

The priest's eyes softened, but his voice grew firm. "You misunderstood my teachings, dear snake. Choosing kindness and refraining from harm doesn't mean allowing yourself to be disrespected. Spirituality is not an invitation to let others mistreat you. Your power is sacred, and part of honoring it is protecting your boundaries."

"But how?" the snake asked, confused.

The priest knelt beside him and spoke with conviction. "You may not bite, but you must hiss. When someone crosses your boundaries, let them know with your 'fizz.' Scare them, warn them—but do not let them forget who you are. Tolerating disrespect is not a virtue; it's self-abandonment. Spirituality requires grace, not submission. Use your power wisely, but never forsake your self-respect."

The snake's dull eyes lit up with a spark of understanding. It was as though the priest's words had breathed life back into its weary soul. "I will remember your words," the snake said. "I will honor my power without causing harm, but I will also demand respect."

As the priest walked away, the snake coiled itself with renewed strength, ready to live in alignment with both kindness and self-worth.

This story is a reminder that your power is not just a gift; it's a responsibility. Practicing kindness does not mean allowing yourself to be diminished. Self-respect is not negotiable. Your boundaries are sacred, and it's your duty to protect them. To show up in the world as your best self, you must honor both your strength and your values.

Remember, choosing grace is powerful, but it's not weakness. Your presence matters, and so does the way you guard it. In every interaction, let your power speak—not to harm, but to command respect.

"True power lies in the courage to be kind without compromising your self-respect. Grace does not mean silence in the face of disrespect—it's the strength to stand tall, hiss if you must, and remain unapologetically you." - Rasesha Rabari

The Fine Line:
Freedom V/S Rebellion

Freedom and rebellion are frequently confused for the same thing. Yet, they are worlds apart. Rebellion is a response, motivated by fury, spite, and an urge to prove to the world that you are not a conformist. It's driven by emotion, and it revels in proving something — usually to other people, but also to yourself. It's a fight against something, an impulse to fight back against perceived limitations.

Freedom, in contrast, is a state of being — serene, intentional and born of self-mastery. Freedom doesn't have to prove anything. It doesn't fight to be noticed. It simply is. It's the capacity to live fully as yourself, independent of external validation or the shackles of ego. Freedom is about choice: choosing what you do, what you believe and what your future holds without outside influence. It is the absolute highest expression of self-worth."

Rebellion may appear bold, but is trapped within opposition. Only by dropping the resistance makes you arrive at your full power and peace. Rebellion is the loud scream of dissatisfaction; freedom is the silent strength of living by your own rules. Freedom is not something to be fought for; it's something to be chosen. And if you've chosen freedom, you've chosen to live fully, authentically, powerfully.

From Survival to Significance

Elevating Your Journey

Imagine shifting from survival to significance. It's not just about improving your circumstances—it's about transforming the way you think, feel, and create. This isn't a surface-level change; it's an inside job, a complete evolution of your emotions, beliefs, and actions.

When you're stuck in survival mode, your inner dialogue sounds like this: "How do I make it through this day?" "How do I pay off this debt?"

But as you rise to stability, success, and finally, significance, your questions change dramatically. Suddenly, you're asking: "What would I like my life to look like five years from now?" "What legacy am I creating?"

This shift demands work. It demands courage. But the rewards? They're monumental.

Problem-Solving to Creating:

In survival mode, your focus is reactive. You want to eliminate problems, stop the bleeding, and find temporary fixes. You're problem-minded. But as you transition to vision-mindedness, you stop asking: "How do I avoid this pain?"

Instead, you ask: "What can I create that didn't exist before?" "What future am I building?"

Individuals who embrace significance don't lack challenges—they face them head-on with an entirely new mindset. They're not rushing from one crisis to another. They're generating solutions, dreaming bigger, and building springboards for the future.

When you're problem-minded, **the goal is subtraction**: Take away the bad. When you're opportunity-minded, **the goal is creation:** Bring forth the good.

This shift unleashes creative energy. It fuels positivity, builds synergy, and makes even challenges feel like stepping stones toward something meaningful.

A Framework: (Survival to Significance)

Survival is necessary—it's our foundation. But staying there is not an option. Let's break it down:

- **Survival (Chaos and Fear)**

   Focus: Reacting.

   Emotions: Victimhood / anxiety.

   Example: "How can I avoid disaster?"

- **Stability (Hope and Knowledge)**

   Focus: Organizing and creating a foundation.

   Emotions: Determination and relief.

   Example: "How can I build a better routine?"

- **Success (Excitement and Confidence)**

  Focus: Setting goals and achieving results.

  Emotions: Pride and inspiration.

  Example: "What can I accomplish next?"

- **Significance (Contribution and Legacy)**

  Focus: Living for something bigger than yourself.

  Emotions: Fulfillment and purpose.

  Example: "What positive impact can I create in the world?"

To transcend survival, your mindset must evolve. Vision-minded people ask, "How do I create abundance, opportunity, and growth?" It's not about perfection—it's about progression.

Breaking Barriers to Action

Release the Brake:

Let's use a metaphor: Picture yourself driving a car. One foot is on the accelerator—your ambitions, goals, and dreams. The other foot? It's stuck on the brake— your fears, anxieties, and doubts.

You're accelerating, but the brake holds you back. Frustrating, isn't it? The solution isn't to push harder on the accelerator—it's to release the brake.

Once you let go of that emotional brake, even small efforts on the accelerator will propel you forward. Fear will no longer sabotage you. Your anxieties will stop slowing you down.

Here's the truth: We all have brakes. Some are labeled fear of failure, others fear of success. Understanding these emotions doesn't just neutralize them—it transforms them into powerful driving forces.

Take a so-called "problem person" in your life. When they're truly listened to, they often become part of the solution. The same applies to your inner struggles. Acknowledge them, understand them, and redirect their energy into something constructive.

Question: Which zone are you stuck in? (Be honest, we're all friends here.)

1. **Survival (Chaos Central):**
   - Tagline: "I'm one coffee spill away from a meltdown."
   - Emotions: Scrambling, anxiety, fear.
   - Mantra: "If it's not on fire, it's not urgent."

2. **Stability (Hopeful Hustler):**
   - Tagline: "At least I know where my keys are."
   - Emotions: Determined but overwhelmed.
   - Mantra: "I'll get through this. Somehow."

3. **Success (Goal Getter):**
   - Tagline: "Look at me, Mom—I'm thriving!"
   - Emotions: Energized, optimistic, maybe a little smug.
   - Mantra: "Next stop: World domination."

4. **Significance (Legacy Builder):**
   - Tagline: "I'm here to change the world—and I brought snacks."

- Emotions: Purposeful, unstoppable.

- Mantra: "It's not about me. It's about what I create."

Pro Tip: If your mantra sounds like a survival movie tagline, it's time to level up.

From Excuses to Action

You don't need the perfect circumstances to move forward. People often think that significance is tied to wealth or external success. Research shows otherwise. **Significance is born out of contribution, not circumstance.**

Driving forces like hope, excitement, and a sense of purpose will push you forward. Restraining forces—fear, victimhood, and escapism—will pull you back.

The question is: Which one are you feeding?
Here's a loud, clear truth: The biggest transformation comes when you switch from reacting to life to creating life.

Survival is necessary, but significance is possible. It's time to take your foot off the brake and start moving toward a life of purpose and abundance.

Wherever you are—whether it's in survival mode or thriving in success—ask yourself: "What's my next step toward creating the life I truly want?"

Your life isn't a problem to solve—it's a masterpiece waiting to be created.

1. *Identify your current mode (survival, stability, success, or significance).*

2. *Release one "brake" this week—fear, procrastination, or self-doubt.*

3. *Create a vision. Not for today, but for the next 10 years.*

The Fine Line: By Choice V/S By Chance:

Life isn't about what happens; it's about what you do and what you make of it. When you live by choice, you take responsibility for your life — you make chosen decisions that reflect your values, your desires, and your purpose.. It's about claiming your power and taking full ownership of your actions, knowing that your choices shape your reality.

When you live by choice, you are the architect of your life. And when you live by choice: you decide your life. You do life intentionally where the future you want is created and every choice is an opportunity to be better. When you live by choice, you are always assessing what you are doing and aligning it with your long-term vision. It's not about trying to control everything—it's about consciously choosing how to respond to the world around you, no matter the circumstances.

On the other hand, living by chance means giving your power away to fate, circumstance, or other people. This is about responding, rather than about producing. If you live by chance, you become passive – a leaf blown through the world, subject to the whims of events outside of your control. Living by chance means you are subject to the whims of life's unpredictability, unable to direct your own course.

Living as we choose is taking back our power over our own destiny. Integrating it is about awareness, hey, you can't control everything, I can control my response, I can control my actions, I can control what I think about. Your choices define your legacy. Make them count.

Understanding Influence and Dynamics

Respect Is Measured by Their Metrics:

When someone asks, "What do you do for a living?" they aren't just curious—they're calculating. They're deciding how much respect to show you. When they ask, "Where do you live?" they're not admiring your address; they're assessing your wealth.

Here's the truth bomb: **you are not defined by their criteria**. Your job title, income, or address do not measure your worth. Your value comes from how you show up in life, the strength of your character, and the courage of your choices. Stop letting others' shallow judgments box you in.

Success isn't about convincing anyone of your value. It's about living a life so authentic, so purpose-driven, that respect is no longer a question—it's inevitable.

Conversations Shape Perceptions:

There are rules for the table and rules for life:

- At a meal with three or more people, **keep private matters private.**

- At a table of five or more, **ditch the business talk and avoid oversharing your personal history.** Why? Because conversations travel faster than you think.

Here's a reality check: **close friends also have close friends**. What you consider a trusted circle might actually be a megaphone to the world. The people who eat together often talk together—and guess what the topic might be? **It's probably you**.

When you understand this, you realize the power of discretion. Guard your words. Protect your energy. **Not everyone deserves access to your life story.**

The Inner Circle:

Your inner circle isn't just a group—it's your fortress. And not everyone gets a key. Surround yourself with people who:

1. **Have grace to love you** – They see your imperfections and love you anyway.

2. **Show compassion to cover you** – They protect your vulnerabilities instead of exposing them.

3. **Possess the capacity to celebrate you** – They cheer for your wins without envy or hesitation.

But steer clear of those who are jealous, divisive, or envious. They are the silent saboteurs, working against you under the guise of friendship. **That's not just unhealthy—it's dangerous.** Your circle should amplify your light, not dim it. Let go of relationships that pull you down or hold you back.

The Broken Mirror

Would you trust a shattered mirror to reflect your true self? Of course not! Broken glass twists the light, distorts your image, and lies about what it sees.

The same is true of broken souls. If you get too close to someone carrying deep wounds and unchecked bitterness, their pain becomes the filter through which they see you. Their frustrations reflect back as distorted judgments, twisting your reality into theirs.

Here's the takeaway: Protect your energy. Don't shrink yourself to cater to someone else's brokenness. You are not responsible for fixing them, and you certainly shouldn't sacrifice your growth to make them comfortable. Stand tall, shine bright, and surround yourself with mirrors that reflect your truth—not their insecurities.

The Gossip and Empty Talk

People have learned how to communicate—they just haven't learned what to communicate. Sharing meaningless chatter, unverified information, or personal drama isn't communication—it's gossip.

Gossip is the currency of small minds. It does nothing to uplift, educate, or empower anyone involved.

And here I repeat it again: **"close friends also have close friends"**. Even your most trusted confidants might unknowingly pass along your words. People love to discuss people. If you give them the material, they'll run with it.

When you speak, ask yourself:

- Does this add value?

- Does this increase knowledge or understanding?

- Does this contribute to growth?

If the answer is no, you're just adding noise.

Spotting the Real from the Fake

Not everyone in your corner is cheering for you. There are two kinds of people in your life:

1. Those who "pray" for your success.

2. Those who "prey" on your struggles.

The hard part? They can look the same on the surface. That's why discernment is critical. You need the wisdom to identify the crowd you're in. Some people show up because they genuinely care; others show up because they've heard what you do and see an opportunity to take advantage of you.

Don't waste time justifying your actions to people who only stick around for your lows. You have a life to build, dreams to chase, and goals to achieve. Your energy is too precious to spend it convincing people who will never see your worth.

Survival mode is reacting to life: chaos, fear, and scrambling for control. Significance is about creating: mission, contribution, and legacy.

When you elevate your mindset, you stop trying to fix what's broken and start focusing on building what's possible. You shift from eliminating problems to creating opportunities. **This isn't just growth—it's transformation.**

1. **Guard Your Inner Circle** – Only let in people who add value, celebrate your wins, and protect your vulnerabilities.

2. **Choose Your Words Wisely** – Speak to educate and empower, not to gossip.

3. **Discern the Crowd Around You** – Spot the difference between those who are for you and those who are simply near you.

4. **Protect Your Energy** – Don't let broken souls or small minds drain your light.

5. **Focus on Creation, Not Correction** – Shift your mindset from fixing the past to building the future.

The Power of Self-Mastery

When Your Heart and Brain Team Up for True Control

When you align with your values, you don't just survive life—you thrive. Your values are the foundation upon which you build your inner peace, integrity, and harmonious relationships. They guide your decisions, protect your energy, and establish boundaries that safeguard your purpose. But here's the truth: your power is not in isolation. It's not about having a heart versus a brain. It's about having the heart and brain working in tandem, each assigned a specific role, bringing you total control and fewer emotional mishaps.

The Catch: Teaming Up Heart and Brain
Here's the genius move: assign your **brain** to handle **professional decisions and boundaries** and your **heart**

to take care of **personal decisions and boundaries**. This allows both sides to focus on what they do best. The brain can structure, analyze, and create strategic boundaries that ensure your work is impactful and productive. Meanwhile, the heart can nurture, love, and forge deep, meaningful personal connections that feed your soul.

But there's a catch— just like any great team, the heart and brain must occasionally step into each other's realms. Your heart should supervise the brain from time to time in **professional matters** to ensure there's no rigidity, no tunnel vision, and that all decisions are aligned with integrity and grace. Likewise, the brain should occasionally supervise the heart's decisions in personal matters to prevent any imbalances—ensuring that you're not being too soft, too lenient, or allowing people to take advantage of your open heart.

In essence, they need to check each other without interference.

This division of labor protects both your emotional world and your professional world, maintaining harmony, clarity, and purpose. When the heart and brain are in sync, you embody true power—one that is built on wisdom, integrity, and respect.

How I Maintain My Peace

Throughout my life, I have learned that maintaining boundaries is the cornerstone of living a meaningful existence. The lines I draw are not just there to protect me—they allow me to live with intention, purpose, and balance. And trust me, there is a profound peace that comes when your heart and brain are working together, with each knowing their place, and both knowing their limits.

One of my rituals is simple, yet powerful. I maintain two circles, one inside the other:

- **The Inner Circle** is reserved for my personal relationships, where only the heart is allowed to rule. Entry to this circle must be earned through values and grace. Anyone who enters this circle and abuses the privilege—by using their **brain** instead of their heart—is politely shown the door. **Yes, you heard it right.**

- **The Outer Circle** is where my professional relationships exist. It's strictly business—my brain is fully engaged here. Yet, there is **zero tolerance for disrespect**. The values I hold dear are not negotiable, no matter the nature of the relationship.

When these circles are respected, life becomes clear. There's peace in knowing where each relationship belongs and how they contribute to your journey.

"In every life, The heart leads the way in love, and the brain paves the way in purpose. But to live in peace, allow them to switch places once in a while, just to keep each other in check." - Rasesha Rabari.

Relationship Dynamic: Dependence vs Codependence

Relationships that rely on interdependent rather than dependent or codependent are healthy. Dependency is part of the human condition; we all need help every once in a while. But dependency becomes unhealthy really, really fast if your whole sense of worth as a person is based on getting approval from someone else, or being in a relationship with someone else. It's the feeling that without this person, you're half a person, an unworthy person, a powerless person.

Codependency – one that really takes this unhealthy dependence a level deeper. It's where you have two people who have done away with their individuality and become entwined in each other's needs, emotions, and desires. A one-sided relationship where a person neglects themselves to cater to the other person's needs at the cost of their own mental or emotional health.

Interdependent relationships involve mutual support and respect. Each person retains their autonomy, their individuality, and their independence. They depend on each other not because doing so is a matter of survival, but because they want to create something larger than either of them could do alone. It is steady, liberating, and leaves space for expansion.

Only with true interdependence growth and harmony can exist. It enables both partners to shine at the same time with unyielding support. Cultivating interdependence creates space for both individuality and deep connection. It's about sharing the journey together without losing yourself in the process.

Your Experience = Your Power

Every mistake, every triumph, every lesson learned—it's all fuel for your growth. Your experience is what sets you apart. Own it.

Are you leveraging your experience to unlock your power?

- Are you constantly learning and adapting?

- Are you stepping into the discomfort of growth?

- Are you using your past to create a better future, or are you letting it hold you back?

When you embrace your experience—flaws and all—you become unstoppable.

Who Are You Really?

To gain control of your life, you need to know your core:

- **Essence**: Who are you at your deepest level?

- **Presence**: How do you show up for others?

- **Power**: What unique impact do you bring to the world?

Write it down. Define it. Own it. Because until you know who you are, you'll never fully step into your power.

Reset:

- Yesterday doesn't matter. What matters is what you do today.

Brainstorming Exercise:

- What can you do differently today?

- Can you adopt one new positive habit?

- Is there someone you've been meaning to reconnect with?

Visualization Exercise:

- Close your eyes and forget who you've been.

- Picture the person you want to become.

- Now, what's one action you can take today to step into that vision?

Your life is a series of fresh starts. Stop dragging yesterday's baggage into today's opportunities.

How to Sharpen Your Skills

Excellence isn't an accident—it's a process. The best in any field didn't just stumble into greatness. They practiced deliberately.

Here's how:

1. **Set specific goals:** What skill do you want to master?

2. **Step out of your comfort zone:** Growth doesn't happen where it's cozy.

3. **Focus deeply**: No distractions. Be present.

4. **Refine constantly**: Work on what needs improvement, not just what you're already good at.

Ask yourself:

- Are you relying on proven techniques?

- Are you creating emotional representations to make the practice stick?

- Are you challenging yourself daily?

Deliberate practice turns potential into power.

Your Inner World

Let's face it—life's going to throw curveballs. But emotional resilience means you won't just survive; you'll thrive.

Signs of emotional resilience:

- You prepare for challenges without fear.

- You commit to your goals regardless of how you feel.

- You learn from failure instead of fearing it. Cultivate gratitude daily. A grateful heart silences negativity and unlocks joy.

Your Wholeness:

Being whole isn't about being perfect—it's about being true.

Ask yourself:

- **Do you know your weaknesses?** Are you working with them instead of against them?

- **Do you live by your core values?** Are your actions aligned with what you believe?

- **Have you identified your zone of genius?** Are you doubling down on your strengths?

- **Are you listening to your intuition?** Or are you ignoring the whispers of your inner wisdom?

Wholeness is about being unapologetically YOU. And guess what? That's enough.

Stop Fooling Yourself:

Let's break it down, no sugarcoating:

- If you're waiting for motivation, you'll be waiting forever.

- If you're avoiding the hard stuff, you're avoiding growth.

- If you're blaming everyone else, you're giving away your power.

Success doesn't knock on your door with a gift basket. It shows up for those who earn it. So stop scrolling, stop whining, and start acting.

Anchoring to Values and Perspective

When Your Values Keep You Grounded

Your power isn't just what you can do—it's how you choose to live. The foundation of your personal power lies in **boundaries, integrity, and self-worth**. It's not about making noise or demanding attention; it's about presence. How you carry yourself in the world sets the tone for every space you occupy. Protecting your peace isn't selfish; it's necessary. **It's the only way to protect your power**. When you honor your boundaries, you honor your soul.

You don't need to control others to maintain your power. **Trust your intuition**. When people fall away, let them. Let them go—because the universe is clearing the path for you. **Trust** is sacred, and it's earned. It's not a "sorry" that can bring it back once broken. When you live with integrity, grace, and purpose, you create a life that uplifts not just you, but everyone around you.

An unintentional life accepts everything and does nothing. An intentional life embraces only what adds to its mission of significance.

Start Small, Dream Big:

Listen up! Life isn't perfect. It shatters your plans, and leaves you holding the broken pieces. But here's the truth: those broken pieces don't define you—unless you let them. Stop staring at the mess and start looking up. Hand your shattered dreams to God, because He's the ultimate architect of comebacks.

Dream big—even when it feels impossible. Why? Because you serve a God who specializes in turning impossibilities into miracles. Start where you are, with what you have, and give it everything you've got.

When you bring your best effort to the table, **God multiplies it.** Your future isn't dictated by your failures or limitations—it's powered by your faith and courage to keep moving forward. **Do the best you can, with what you've got, and watch God handle the rest.**

This is your moment. Don't just live—**create a life that matters**. Dream. Build. Thrive. Because when you align your vision with His power, the extraordinary happens.

The Fine Line:
Escape V/S Experience

We all have moments when we want to escape—when life feels too hard, too overwhelming, or too painful. But there's a **big difference** between escaping and truly experiencing life.

Escape is about avoidance. It's about running from your problems, your emotions, or your responsibilities. It's finding distractions or numbing yourself to keep the pain or discomfort at bay. Whether it's through substance abuse, mindless entertainment, or numbing routines, escape keeps you stuck in a cycle of avoidance and stagnation. **Escape is a temporary fix**, but it never heals the underlying issues.

Experience, however, is about embracing life fully, even in its discomfort. It's about stepping into the present moment and allowing yourself to feel, learn, and grow through whatever comes your way. Experience means facing challenges head-on, knowing that you are strong enough to handle whatever arises. Life isn't about avoiding the storm—it's about dancing in the rain.

When you choose to experience life, you gain wisdom, resilience, and a deeper understanding of yourself and the world around you. You learn to process emotions, face your fears, and rise above them. Every challenge becomes an opportunity to grow stronger, wiser, and more connected to your true self.

Do It Anyway: I am highly influenced by this quote and I live by it.

People are often unreasonable, illogical, and self-centered. **Forgive them anyway**.

If you are kind, people may accuse you of selfishness or ulterior motives. **Be kind anyway.**

If you are successful, you will win some false friends and some true enemies. **Succeed anyway.**

If you are honest and frank, people may cheat you. **Be honest and frank anyway**.

What you spend years building, someone could destroy overnight. **Build anyway**.

If you find serenity and happiness, they may be jealous. **Be happy anyway**.

The good you do today, people will often forget tomorrow. **Do good anyway.**

Give the world the best you have, and it may never be enough. **Give your best anyway.**

You see, in the final analysis, it is between you and your God. **It was never between you and them anyway. -Mother Terasa**

Let me be clear: **You matter**. You matter in every decision you make, every action you take, and every soul you touch. The road to fulfillment, success, and inner peace? It's not always easy—hell, sometimes it's downright brutal—but hear me loud and clear: **it is always worth it.**

I wrote this book for one reason—"**YOU**". For the person who is ready to grab life by the reins, take full ownership of their choices, and step unapologetically into their power.

Your choices matter. Your relationships matter. YOUR LIFE MATTERS.

But here's the real deal: the most important relationship you'll ever have is the one you have with yourself. When you trust yourself, when you honor your values, and when you choose your path with intention, something incredible happens. **You stop living by default and start living by design.**

This is your moment to own your power. Your essence, your presence, your influence—it's all within you, waiting to be unleashed. So lean in, show up, and never forget: **You are the architect of a life that truly matters.**

Let's do this.

— I will always Believe in You.

"The world may not always understand your journey, but your soul does. When you choose authenticity over approval, peace over chaos, and love over fear, you align yourself with a purpose far greater than anything the world can offer." - Rasesha Rabari

Taking Purposeful Action 18.

Your Daily Power Playbook

Hey, superstar..!! Always remember :You're not a passenger—you're the driver.

This isn't just another "to-do" list; it's your power-up list. Think of it as daily emotional armor, a roadmap to rediscovering the incredible YOU.

1. **Wake Up Like a Boss**

    Seriously, if your first thought is "I can't," flip it to "What's one thing I can OWN today?" Then, go crush it.

2. **Hydrate Like You're Part Cactus**

    No, coffee doesn't count (sorry). Water is life, and hydrated you = happier you.

3. Stretch It Out

Not just your body—your mindset. Can you push one boundary today? Physically, emotionally, or mentally?

4. Call Out the Comparison Game

Scrolling Instagram thinking everyone's life is better than yours? Don't tell me you're buying that highlight reel nonsense. Celebrate your lane.

5. Breathe Like You Mean It

Anxiety creeping in? Stop. Inhale for 4. Hold for 4. Exhale for 4. You're welcome.

6. Turn Stress into a Sprint

Got a big problem? Break it into mini wins. Big progress is just tiny victories stacked like pancakes.

7. Laugh at Your Inner Critic

Seriously, that voice telling you you're not enough? It's a drama queen. Don't let it run the show.

8. Phone a Friend—Not Just to Vent

Call someone who lifts you up, not just to unload. Connection is the antidote to isolation.

9. Dance It Out

Yep, in your kitchen, in your pajamas. No judgment. Movement = instant mood boost.

10. Set Boundaries Like a Pro

Got energy vampires? Say "no" with love, and protect your peace.

11. Let It Go (No Frozen Sing-Along Required)

Angry at someone? Holding onto it is like drinking poison and expecting them to get sick. Release it—for you.

12. Own Your Mistakes, But Don't Marry Them

Made a mess? Cool. Learn, clean up, and move forward. You're not your screw-ups.

13. Journal Your Wins

Big or small, write them down. Didn't yell at traffic today? Boom. Win.

14. Reclaim Your Mirror

Don't tell me you're still letting society dictate how you see yourself. Stand tall. You're incredible.

15. Cook Something That Makes You Smile

Even if it's grilled cheese. Nourish your body and your soul.

16. Unplug Like Your Sanity Depends on It

Because, spoiler alert—it does. Log off, breathe in real life, and reconnect.

17. Schedule Joy Like It's a Meeting

Fun isn't optional; it's essential. Put it in your calendar and show up for it.

18. Face a Fear Head-On

Afraid to fail? Good. That's where the growth happens. Take one small step toward it today.

19. Stop Apologizing for Existing

Did you bump into someone, and they said sorry first? Don't tell me you're apologizing back for breathing. Own your space.

20. Prioritize Sleep Like It's Gold

Because it is. Set a bedtime, put down the phone, and let your body recharge.

21. Gratitude Check-In

Name three things you're thankful for today. Even if it's just good coffee or the fact you didn't spill it.

22. Give Yourself Permission to Suck at Something

First draft, first workout, first anything—it's not supposed to be perfect. Just start.

23. Ask for Help Without Shame

Need support? Say it. Asking isn't weakness; it's strength.

24. Declutter Something

Your desk, your mind, your Netflix queue. Clarity starts with space.

25. Stop Waiting for the "Perfect Moment"

Newsflash: it's not coming. It starts to get messy. Start now.

26. Smile at a Stranger

They might need it as much as you do. Plus, it's free.

27. Celebrate Progress Over Perfection

Took a baby step? Amazing. Keep going. Progress > perfection every time.

28. Redefine Failure as Feedback

Didn't go as planned? Cool. What's the lesson? Use it, grow, repeat.

29. Visualize Tomorrow's Win

Before bed, imagine one thing you'll crush tomorrow. Then wake up and make it happen.

30. Remember: You're Worth It

Don't tell me you're doubting that. You matter. Full stop. Believe it, and live like it.

Hey, YOU!

Thank you for investing your time, energy, and heart into this book. It means the world to me that you've chosen to take this journey, not just for yourself, but for the life you're creating and the people you're impacting along the way.

Let me be real with you: this book is a tool—a spark. But the fire? That's all you. It's your commitment, your focus, and your action that will determine how far you go. **So use this book, use the action guide, and show up for yourself every single day.**

My deepest hope is that you become the hero of your own story. That you step boldly into your power, shatter the limits you thought you had, and achieve everything your heart desires. The world needs what only YOU can bring, so don't hold back.

I can't wait to see the incredible life you create. I'm rooting for you, every step of the way. If you have questions or want to share your wins (or even your struggles), I'd love to hear from you.

- Connect with me on Facebook: *(Insert Link)*
- Follow me on Instagram: *(Insert Link)*

Here's to your journey, your growth, and the unstoppable force that is YOU.

Let's go make magic happen.

With gratitude and belief in you,

Rasesha Rabari

Author of "*I Believe You Matter*"